"*The Pleasures of Exile* as a Counter-Discourse: George Lamming's Deconstruction of

The Tempest and Reconstruction of the Caribbean Identity"

Author

Md. Abdul Karim Ruman

MA in English, Jahangirnagar University, Bangladesh

Lecturer, Department of English, University of Bisha, KSA

1

Authorship Statement

I do, hereby, declare that the dissertation is done by my own. This is not plagiarized, and all the references used here, except some common knowledge, are duly acknowledged in MLA style. Again, this research paper is not free from limitations. There might be some minor mistakes such as typing mistakes, British/American spellings and mechanics etc., despite my utmost care. I must apologize for that, and I would like to appreciate any kind of constructive criticism regarding my research.

Table of Contents

Abstract

The Pleasures of Exile is a postcolonialist, postrealist and postnationalist counter-discourse because it gives us George Lamming's glimpse of the complex issues of identity contained within the Caribbean island-states that were largely shaped by European colonial practice from the late-fifteenth century upto the late twentieth century. My research questions are—"How are the nations of the Caribbean and/or the West Indies originated? How are they represented by canonical discourses and how is their identity constructed? What about its impact throughout different times and spaces? Is it possible to deconstruct and reconstruct their identity through counter-discourse?"—with a view to exploring George Lamming's endeavour in *The Pleasures of Exile* to answer these questions with fact and fiction. The uprooting of the natives and importation of African slaves to toil in sugar plantations, the introduction of Indian and Chinese indentured labourers to replace African slaves after the abolition of slavery, as well as the presence of European colonisers led to the creation of hybrid Caribbean communities of immigrants or exiled people, all with broken cultures and history. I would like to establish that as the canonical discourses like *The Tempest*, the B.B.C. etc. construct the Caribbean's mythologized identities negatively with biased perspectives for their colonial 'civilizing mission', Lamming has tried to deconstruct or decentralize their canonical position counter-discursively to reconstruct his national identity. I have also focused on the problems of the Caribbean hyphenated identities that imply double heredity. So, the region seems to be a no man's land where people lack an autonomous and homogenous identity. At the end of my research, I have tried to establish that—by reviewing colonial history, dismantling the textual unconscious of *The Tempest* as a poststructuralist critic and rejecting the stereotype identities created by other legitimizing Western discourses, Lamming's *The Pleasures of Exile* functions as a counter-discursive signifier of the post-

4

colonial Caribbean's metamorphosis into some cross-cultural identities, identities that are experienced between the Caribbean and the West.

Introduction

Since the time of the Great Discoveries and the globalization of our planet, identities are more than ever flying, shifting, changing places and forms, moving around numerous locations. The colonial circumstances complicated the racial, socio-political and cultural relations and constitute an indisputable turning point in the development of the countries involved. As Edouard Glissant reminds us in *Caribbean Discourse*, the answer to the question of "What is the Caribbean?"--is "a multiple series of relationships". My hypothesis concerning the Caribbean scenario is that--*The Pleasures of Exile* is a postcolonialist, postrealist and postnationalist counter-discourse because it gives us George Lamming's glimpse of the complex issues of identity contained within the Caribbean island-states that were largely shaped by European colonial discourse and practice from the late fifteenth century until the late twentieth century. Geographically, 'the Caribbean' refers to all island nations of the Caribbean Sea and territories on the surrounding South and Central American mainland, while 'West Indies' refers only to the formerly British colonies. Whatever, the complexities are entailed in the process of trying to represent its diverse people with a diverse history with a homogenous, autonomous 'identity'. According to Michel Foucault, our identity is constructed by how we are seen. From this perspective, 'the Caribbean identity' refers to how people in the world see and evaluate the Caribbean, either individually or globally, and the ways that it is politically, culturally and discursively constructed along with the possibility of reconstruction. So my research questions are—"How are the nations of the Caribbean and/or the West Indies originated? How are they represented by canonical discourses and how is their identity constructed? What about its impact throughout different times and spaces of the world? Is it possible to deconstruct and reconstruct their identity through counter-discourse?" In *The Pleasures of Exile* (1960), George Lamming explores their answers to assert a dignified identity of the Caribbean people.

First, we have to keep in mind that since 1960s there has been a great emphasis on decolonization and emergent nationalism throughout the Caribbean region. Concerning their background, of all the post-colonial peoples only the Caribbean can be said to be largely dispossessed of their history and identity due to rootlessness, dispossession, diaspora and hybridity. The Caribs and the Arawaks, the original dwellers of the islands still remain as a ghostly trace on its modern creolized inhabitants. So, the objective of my research is to explore, with textual signifiers, Lamming's dealing with the themes of colonial history of displacement and dispossession, slavery and racial subjugation, decolonization and the Caribbean emigrant experiences as a quest for deconstruction and reconstruction of his national identity. I would like to establish that as the canonical discourses like *The Tempest*, the B.B.C. etc. construct the Caribbean's mythologized identities negatively with biased perspectives for their own benefits, Lamming has tried to deconstruct or decentralize their canonical position counter-discursively. But according to Derrida, every experience has more than one interpretations that must be subjective, perspectival and biased; and subjectivity denies authenticity. In that sense, no work can claim a universal meaning to 'the Caribbean identity'. However, Lamming's quest can be called his intellectual commitment to his land and people "who are still regarded [by Europe and America] as the unfortunate descendants of languageless and deformed slaves" (119).

The essays of *The Pleasures of Exile* (1960) are written on the basis of imagination and experience. It represents the critical issues like the Caribbean pre-colonial and colonial situations leading to the nation's struggle for decolonization and Lamming's post-colonialist vision; history of diasporas and slavery; racism, hybridity and identity crisis; politics of language, religion, canonical discourses, media, Ideological and Repressive State Apparatuses etc.--in the construction, representation and manipulation of the Caribbean's stereotype identities and their worldwide impacts. And in that sense, the book emerges as Lamming's revisioning and rewriting the Caribbean colonial history from a post-colonial perspective. Lamming once said—

> From about the beginning of sixties, I entered into the [Trinidad] region not just as
> witness and observer, but in a certain kind of activist and ... as the New World Group
> ... [who] talked about the Caribbean as it reacted to colonial power and so on. We

saw the independence of Guyana not as a Guyanese affair. This was a matter that concerned the whole region.

Indeed, George Lamming wants literature of the region to be part of the consciousness of the Caribbean. Therefore, besides focusing on the personal experiences, he also (re)tells the ethnic and social history of his nation. In fact, to have more reliable version of a nation's history, we need some historiographer from inside the very territory. From this perspective, Lamming emerges as a Caribbean voice to deconstruct the colonial negative versions of the Caribbean history and identity, and to explore, restore and rewrite the positive ones. I would try to prove my viewpoint that as a part of his counter-discursive quest, Lamming attempts a postcolonial allegorical reading of Shakespeare's *The Tempest* to dismantle or expose the British colonial ideology before the world.

The methodology adopted in my research consists of a close intertextual and comparative analysis, which will draw from interdisciplinary theoretical frameworks, taking a critical exploration mainly towards the Caribbean postcolonial identity. I would focus on how Lamming reworks the European 'classics' to invest them with more local relevance and to divest them of their assumed authority/authenticity. Helen Tiffin terms such a project as 'canonical counter-discourse', a process whereby a post-colonial writer unveils and dismantles the basic assumptions of a specific canonical text by developing a 'counter' text that preserves many of the identifying signifiers of the original while altering, often allegorically, its structure of power. Many of the approaches used here have been borrowed from the concepts of several postcolonial and cultural critics, such as Stuart Hall, Bill Ashcroft, Helen Tiffin, Michel Foucault, Edward Said, Salman Rushdie, Louise Althusser, Frantz Fanon, W.E.B. Du Boise, N'gugi, Walcott and others--that will throw light on important debates which have featured in post-colonial and cultural theories in recent times; some textual references involved directly or indirectly with the Caribbean identity. In order to prove my hypothesis, I would also use some extracts from historical sources; because the extracts serve to remind us that the determining condition of postcolonial cultures is the historical phenomena of colonialism, with its range of material practices and effects mentioned above. And these material conditions and their relationship to questions of ideology and representation are at the heart of the most vigorous debates.

Therefore, I would try to locate from this text the necessary postcolonial and cultural issues relevant to my hypothesis. To elaborate and support my argument, the five chapters of this dissertation are organized around this paradigm. Chapter I is about the Caribbean background. Chapter II consists of a theoretical framework on the issues related to post-colonial and cultural identity. In chapter III, I have focused on the politics of representing the Caribbean in colonial-discourses as well as the ideological resistance to those mythical stereotyping. Then chapter IV concentrates on Lamming's Deconstruction of canonical-discourse *The Tempest* & reconstruction of the Caribbean identity through allegory. In the final chapter, Lamming's quest for his contemporary Caribbean identity in real life situations throughout the world is presented with textual references. And the terms or terminologies associated with 'identity' are incorporated in every relevant section. As regards the mode of argument, I have tried to relate Shakespeare's discourse *The Tempest* and Lamming's counter-discourse *The Pleasures of Exile* to the Caribbean historical circumstances which produced them and in which they have been read. So I have placed them in postcolonial critical context, concentrating on Lamming's reinterpretation of a colonial canon by breaking fresh ground of Western outlook/argument. That is, I have made cultural and political reading of them. The primary sources like historical documents, Lamming's works and interview etc. and the secondary sources like books and articles on postcolonial and cultural issues are cited at the end of my research. I think that since very little research has so far been done on *The Pleasures of Exile*, my critical-analytical approach may have some importance; at the same time, some limitations. After all, my conviction is that--my research would engage the readers with a vast scope of existing knowledge and debates on the Caribbean postcolonial identity.

Chapter I

The Caribbean Background:

The Historical and Cultural Scenario

In an interview at the East Coast of Barbados in 1989, George Lamming said, "We had grown up without that dimension [making the Caribbean history a reality] and then not only as a writer of something about capitalism and slavery, but actual articulator in person, bringing together of young people to look at documents". Indeed, the colonial historical perspectives have inextricably determined the identity of the Caribbean nation. In other words, identity is the product of history; on the personal level, of memory. In a lecture delivered at Columbia University in April 1971, Walcott said that for the Caribbean writers—

> History is fiction, subject to a fitful muse, memory'; and servitude to this muse 'has produced a literature ... of revenge written by the descendants of slaves ... this literature serves historical truth ... The truly tough aesthetic of the New World neither explains nor forgives history ... The shipwrecks ... of the crew in *The Tempest* are the end of an Old World ...

Again, according to Christopher O'Reilly, the Caribbean is a unique nation in that its original inhabitants, the Amerindian Arawaks and the Caribs no longer inhabit the area. Diseases and direct military oppression wiped them out when the European began to occupy the islands in the sixteenth century. Especially, the nations of the Caribbean have been associated with the British for over three hundred years, first as slave societies, then as colonies, and now as members of the Commonwealth. Though traces of Carib culture and language still exist, the Caribbean today is a mixture of the various races and cultures. This includes diasporic people and traditions from Europe, Africa, India, China etc.

Sugar Islands and the creation of slave colonies:

The practice of enslaving peoples of other political, racial or ethnic backgrounds, as repulsive as it is to us today, is of great antiquity and was common to most, if not all, of the high civilizations of the Old World. The present Caribbean population is for the most part the consequences of the deliberate or forced migration of people from different parts of the world for different purposes. To be specific, the most important factor in the creation of Caribbean societies was the establishment of sugar plantations worked first by exploited African slaves and subsequently by Asian indentured labourers, once the indigenous labour force had been wiped out. Their numbers are still disputed. For instance, a conservative estimate puts the number of slaves transported across the Atlantic between 1450 and 1900 at 11,698,000. It has been estimated that fewer than half of the slaves captured actually survived the journey across the notorious middle passage of six thousand miles due to extreme overcrowding, trauma, starvation, contaminated food and water, appalling sanitation and diseases etc. Indeed, this largest forced migration in the world history can be called a process of systematic dehumanization. In the Caribbean islands, they were catalogued, treated and tortured as working animals, even to the extent that the strongest were used to warn them about any impending revolt.

According to *Encyclopedia of Post-colonial Literatures in English*, when Christopher Columbus first arrived in the Caribbean island, in the last decade of the fifteenth century, the region was inhabited by Taino peoples—Arawaks and Caribs—to whom the European applied the misnomer Indian, or Amerindian. It did not take long for the Spaniards, in the name of the Bible, of the king of Spain, and of elusive gold, to all but eliminate these original islanders, whether through forced labour or by the sword and gun. Other European nations—English, French and Dutch—followed the Spaniards into the Caribbean and in many places supplanted them. For instance, Jamaica came under British sovereignty in 1655 and became the hub of the slave trade in the area. Further, some smaller migrations, in some cases occasioned by religious persecution—from Portugal, Spain, and the Middle East—have also been appreciable, however small the numbers, in the making of the Caribbean nation. Therefore, the socio-cultural West Indian countries vary today partly as a function of the mixture of

European colonizing influences to which each was subjected. With the extinction of the indigenous people went the extinction of indigenous languages and their replacement by imported cultural varieties. It led to their identity crisis.

The foundations of modern West Indian society were laid by this enforced and purely expedient encounter of Africa, Asia and Europe in the Caribbean islands. In evidence, the process of slavery had profound effects upon the psychology and cultures of them. Manipulation of religion is an important example of it. Clawson states that the purposes of the Spaniards, Portuguese and the English in coming to the New World centred on the so-called "three G's: Gold, God and Glory". Since the slaves were branded and baptized at the port cities after their arrival, it was alleged that slavery delivered them into the cherishing hands of Christian masters. Thus, their original religion was also lost and it led to a significant aspect of the Caribbean identity crisis.

Again, slaves had few rights and little control over their lives. They often wore padlocked collars, and were frequently mistreated. They were not allowed to learn how to read or write. Owners could treat them cruelly—starving, beating, or even killing them. Murder of a slave by a white was not a capital felony in Barbados, e.g., until 1805. Barbados Law prescribed 'a moderate whipping' for absence from a plantation without leave, runaways were to be taken 'alive or dead'. Those absent for more than 30 days were liable to the death penalty. Colonial slave codes were all broadly similar. After being captured and torn forever from their loved ones, slaves lost their individuality and identity.

To justify all brutalities, the usual arguments in the name of 'civilizing mission' were advanced through colonial canonical discourses of travellers, churchmen, historians, writers and philosophers (e.g., Hume) to establish the inherent inferiority of the Caribbean black race that appeared to be the white men's burden. Unfortunately this meant that whatever the whites would do, would be regarded in any way as 'civilized'; and whatever the blacks would do, would be represented as 'savagery'. In this regard, Aime Cessaire writes in *Discourse on Colonialism*—"Between colonizer and colonized, there is room only for forced labour, intimidation, pressure, the police ... compulsory crops, contempt, mistrust, arrogance … brainless elites, degraded masses" (177). In *The Pleasures of Exile*, George Lamming reveals that the common objective of the empires in the Caribbean was exploitation in the interest of the metropolitan core.

Meanwhile, it is universal that when power corrupts, resistance erupts. Lamming revisits that "the great ambition of the slaves was to be free. They had fought and died to achieve it. The spirit which demanded it had transformed men who lived like brutes into soldiers of considerable intelligence and daring" (138).

After the British abolished slavery in 1833 a large number of the Asian and the African were imported to form the labour force and consequently to add to the ethnic and cultural hybridity of the Caribbean. Then the colonial policy of 'divide and rule' comes to the surface, as Lamming scrutinizes: "The old imperialism of Europe, appropriating the destiny of the region through a strategy of fragmentation by language (French West Indies, British West Indies, Dutch, Spanish West Indies, and so on) has given way to a new and more fearsome thrust of imperial encirclement" (8).

However, local agitations compelled the British colonizers to grant the Caribbean some internal self-government in the 1940s and then, inevitably, to independence, except for one or two of the smallest islands. And, we have to keep in mind Lamming's reference to the context: "There were no independent countries in the English-speaking Caribbean when I started to write *The Pleasures of Exile* in 1959" (Introduction to 1984 edition). So, his mission was decolonization and vision was freedom.

To conclude this part, the European imperial enterprise ensured that the worst features of colonialism throughout the globe would all be combined in the Caribbean area. In brief, the history of the Caribbean is about 30 million people scattered across an arc of islands—Jamaica, Haiti, Barbados, Antigua, Martinique, Trinidad; among others—separated by the languages and cultures of their colonizers, but joined together, nevertheless, by a common subaltern heritage. For whether French, English, Spanish, or latterly American, the nationality of their masters has made only a notional difference to the peoples of the Caribbean. So we can say that the Caribbean identity is a problematic and hotchpotch identity. And the Caribbean history is not about root, but about route. However, *The Pleasures of Exile* comes as a result of Lamming's protest against the brutality of the Europeans by picturing the illegal practice they were doing over the Caribbean.

Chapter II

Theoretical Framework on Post-colonial Identity:

The aim of this chapter is to explore some (political and cultural) implications of nationalist projects in post-colonial societies and examine the extent of national identity. In colonial time and space, identities are based on partial traits (skin colour, socio-economic status, nationality or ethnicity, region, profession, generation and so on). And the relative weight of identities changes across time and space. Besides, the terms by which identities are ascribed are determined by power relations, depending on who is using it and in what context. For instance, media industries accelerate identity formation by quickly targeting particular identities as specific. Consequently, contemporary cultural and postcolonial theories seek to challenge or deconstruct the essentialist and universalizing identities.

For instance, in "Cultural Identity and Diaspora", the Caribbean writer Stuart Hall states that identity is not as transparent or unproblematic as we think. We should think of identity as a 'production' that is never complete, always in process, and always constituted within, not outside, representation. This view problematises the very authority and authenticity to which the term 'cultural identity' lays claim. Our cultural identities reflect the common historical experiences and shared cultural codes that provide us, as 'one people', with stable, unchanging and continuous frames of reference and meaning, beneath the shifting divisions and vicissitudes of our actual history. This 'oneness', underlying all the other, more superficial differences, is the truth, the essence, of 'Caribbeanness', of the black experience. It is this identity which a Caribbean or black diaspora must discover, unearth, bring to light and express through discursive representation. Now I would like to proceed with a key concept on 'diaspora'.

'Diaspora' is a Greek word meaning 'to disperse'. In the post-colonial context, diaspora refers to forcible or voluntary migration of people from their homelands to new regions. Thus, it is a central historical fact of displacement during colonization. A question that I assume may come to the reader's mind is: 'Why and how have the diasporas occurred in the Caribbean context?'

To make the concepts of diaspora and displacement more clearly, I would like to define four terminologies related to the identity of the diasporic people. First is 'Settler', one who settles in a new country, i.e., the colonists who settled in the Caribbean as resident. Second is 'migrant', a person who moves or who is made to move from one place to another, especially in order to find work. For example, the African people who were transported as slaves, or the Indian and the Chinese people as indentured labour--to the Caribbean sugar plantations are migrants. Third is 'immigrant', a person who comes to live permanently in a place or country from other country in legal and technical processes. Fourth is 'exile', a person who is living in a foreign country, usually for political reasons. But in Lamming's work, the Caribbean writers' exile in England was an exploration for identity.

'Hybridity' is integrated with the Caribbean diasporic context. People from different countries appeared here and out of their inter-racial marriages came up a nation called 'the Caribbean'. Thus, 'the Caribbean' is a hybridized form of different geographical identities including the European, the African, the American, the Spanish, the East Indian, the Chinese, the Portuguese and the Dutch. By identity we here refer to national or political identity, which is based on the Caribbean's cultural heritage and political habitation. In the last chapter, I would illustrate Lamming's observation on the Caribbean 'hybrid identity' as a "newly composed, mixed or contradictory" identity; a new form out of different or unlike trend. Hybridity takes many forms in the scenario: cultural, political, racial etc. Now, its meanings has been extended to refer to the hyphenated identities of persons or ethnic communities; e.g., the Afro-Caribbean. The ethnic mixture suggests a homogeneity that results not merely from amalgamation, but also an assimilation that destroys the Caribbean identity.

Again, when a black marries a white, their children share both black and white blood; and the identity of these mulattos is hybrid as well. In each case, hybridity leads to existential (identity) crisis as a malaise. However, the Caribbean postcolonial writers attempt to show hybridity as an anti-colonial tool regarding their identity and culture, because in hybridity the sense of mixing breaks down the strict polarization of imperialism. That is why, in *The Pleasures of Exile,* there is a critical awareness of the Caribbean origin and a willingness to acknowledge the African, Asian and Chinese legacy as part and parcel of their national identity.

Now, in post-colonial societies, the rediscovery of identity is often the object of what Frantz Fanon once called a "passionate research ... directed by the secret hope of discovering beyond the misery of today, beyond self-contempt, resignation and abjuration, some very beautiful and splendid era whose existence rehabilitates us both in regard to ourselves and in regard to others". He also says, "Colonialism is not satisfied merely with holding a people in its grip and emptying the native's brain of all form and content. By a kind of perverted logic, it turns to the past of oppressed people, and distorts, disfigures and destroys it". Therefore, Lamming quests for reviving the Caribbean history as a commitment by understanding--how the rift of separation, the 'loss of identity', which has been integral to the Caribbean experience, only begins to be healed when these forgotten connections are once more set in place. He attempts to reconstruct in discursive terms the underlying unified identity of the black Caribbean people. In this regard, *The Pleasures of Exile* is a resource of resistance and identity, with which to confront and reform the Western representations of the Caribbean.

Again, Stuart Hall states that identities are the names we give to the different ways we are positioned by, and position ourselves within, the narratives of the past. It is only from this position that we can properly understand the traumatic character of the 'colonial experience'. The Caribbean have been positioned, subjected and constructed as different and other, in Said's sense of *Orientalism*, within the categories of knowledge of the West by the dominant regimes of representation. In this aspect, discourse designates a form of representation. And, the canonical discourses had the power to make the Caribbean see 'other' with dire consequences. Equally important, every regime of representation is a regime of power formed, as Foucault reminds us, by the fatal couplet 'power/ knowledge'. But this kind of knowledge is internal, not external. It is one thing to position a subject or set of peoples as the 'other' of a dominant discourse that is reinforced by education, law and media. To Foucault, discursive practices establish what is accepted as 'reality' in a given society.

In Helen Tiffin's view, post-colonial cultures are inevitably hybridized, involving a dialectical relationship between European ontology and epistemology and the impulse to create or recreate independent local identity. Decolonization is a process that invokes an ongoing dialectic between hegemonic centrist system and peripheral subversion of them, between European or British discourses and their post-colonial dis/mantling. In *Culture and Imperialism*, Edward Said situates Lamming as one of the key figures in the transition from colonization to decolonization, and his work as belonging to a body of 'resistance culture'. But as it is not possible to create or recreate national or regional formations wholly independent of his colonial enterprise, it has been his project to interrogate European discourses and discursive strategies from a privileged position within (and between) two worlds; to investigate the means by which Europe imposed and maintained its codes in the colonial domination of so much of the rest of the world; specifically the Caribbean. Now to clarify 'discourse' in Foucault's term, it is the system of knowledge by which the world can be known. Discourse has played an important role in constituting identity.

18

In contrast, Post-colonial counter-discursive strategies involve a mapping of the dominant discourse, a rereading of its underlying assumptions, and the (dis)mantling of these assumptions from the cross-cultural standpoint of the imperially subjectified 'local'. Thus the rereading and rewriting of the European historical and fictional records are vital and inescapable tasks for the Caribbean intellectuals, who seem to be identical with the demonstration of Stephen Slemon that the potential of allegory is a privileged site of anti-colonial or post-colonial discourse. For instance, Shakespeare's *The Tempest* is often considered to be a colonial discourse, a part of the process of 'fixing' relations between Europe and its 'others', of establishing patterns of reading alterity at the same time as it inscribed the 'fixity' of that alterity, naturalizing difference within its own cognitive codes. But the function of such a canonical text at the colonial periphery also becomes an important part of material imperial practice, in that, through educational and critical institutions, it continually displays and repeats for the colonized subject, the original capture of his/her alterity and the processes of its annihilation, marginalization, or naturalization as if this were axiomatic, culturally ungrounded, 'universal', natural. Hence, the politics of discourse is that it constructs identity through fantasy, narrative and myth.

It is to note that long before the theoretical elevation of counter-discursivity as a paradigm of postcolonial writing, Lamming's essays insist on the counter-discursivity as a necessary legacy of the colonial encounter. This legacy, rooted as it is in language and discourse, can be appropriated, revised and transformed only within the context of a systematic questioning and dismantling of imperial codes of governance, culture, and self-fashioning that permeate European writing. We can locate some counter-discursive features from *The Pleasures of Exile*. For example, with the reversal of master-slave hierarchy in "The African Presence" Lamming has a decentralizing or subversive portrayal of--the Nigerian Minister's undersecretary as a servile Englishman, his black wife as the mistress of the English wife whose children studying in England have no warning that their "Daddy has lost his crown" (177). Besides, he degrades the colonizers and upgrade the colonized ancestors' ('Nigeria was mine' p.175) new role in this visionary context: "African are not anti-English or anti-European. They ask simply that Prospero must be transformed, rejuvenated, and ultimately restored to his original condition of a man among men" (178). It establishes the Caribbean as liberal.

Survey or Review on the Caribbean Identity:

For Foucault and Lacan, identity is a signifier at play in cultural fields of individuals. And in Kobena Mercer's view, identity becomes an issue when something assumed to be fixed, coherent and stable--is displaced by the experience of doubt and uncertainty. From their perspectives, the project to establish an autonomous and homogenous identity in the pluralistic immigrant Caribbean society where there is no single notion of 'Caribbeanness' but a growing acceptance of syncretic model that is inclusive and accepts the diversity and hybridity as the foundation of identities--is probably more problematic, uncertain and fraught than in the other post-colonial societies. The dispossession and displacement that the uprooted, marginalized, Diasporic Caribbean people are subjected to, bring them into a state of agony and identity crisis. As a highly political author, Lamming is credited, along with Vic Reid, Wilson Harris, V.S. Naipaul, Everton Weekes, Derek Walcott, Garfield Sobers, Mighty Sparrow, and others, with making the emergence of a Caribbean identity possible. Lamming sees the lack of cultural identity in this region as a direct result of the history of colonial rule.

In a wondrous introduction to Party Politics in the West Indies, C. L. R. James, one of the most distinguished thinkers of the modern Caribbean, made the following statement about the people of the Anglophone Caribbean:

> People of the West Indies, you do not know your own power. No one dares to tell you. You are a strange, a unique combination of the greatest driving force in the world today, the underdeveloped formerly colonial coloured peoples; and more than any of them, by education, way of life and language, you are completely part of Western civilization ... All those who would say or imply that you are in any way backward and therefore cannot in a few years become a modern advanced people are your enemies, satisfied with the positions that they hold and ready to keep you where you are forever.

It is noticeable that James made this statement in 1961, just one year after the publication of *The Pleasures of Exile.* Because while one can and may speak of a Caribbean experience or a Caribbean identity, it is necessary to be aware of the nuances of each specific experience and how it played out in the region. Indeed, because of its supposed humanistic functions, 'English Literature' occupied a privileged position in the colonial classroom, where its study was designed to 'civilise' native students by inculcating in them British tastes and values, regardless of the exigencies of the local context. [2]

According to Stuart Hall, we might think of the black Caribbean identities as 'framed' by two axes or vectors, simultaneously operative: the vector of similarity and continuity; and the vector of difference and rupture. Caribbean identities always have to be thought of in terms of the dialogic relationship between these two axes. The one gives us some grounding in, some continuity with, the past. The second reminds us that what we share is precisely the experience of a profound discontinuity: the peoples dragged from African and Asian subcontinents; and it 'unified' these people across their differences, in the same moment as it cut them off from direct access to their past.

In addition, since the Western discourses normalize and appropriate Africa by freezing it into some timeless zone of the primitive, unchanging past--Hall inspires that Africa must be reckoned with by the Caribbean people. It seems that in his urge and search for root, Lamming emerges as such a Caribbean spokesman in "Ishmael at Home" of *The pleasures of Exile*:

> We need an Institute of African and Oriental Studies right in the heart of Port-of-Spain. In this institute we will ask for some light on what has been discovered of the African civilizations before the European arrival. For West Indians, on the whole, still have to learn that Africa existed—not simply as desert, river and malaria—but as a home where men were alive and engaged in a human struggle with nature. The presence of some Africans in the Caribbean will help to dislodge that image of Africa as bush and artless nature, an image which prospero planted most successfully in the West Indian consciousness. (155)

It belongs irrevocably, for them, to what Edward Said once called an "imaginative geography and history". Their belongingness of it constitutes what Benedict Anderson too calls 'an imagined community'. Again, none of the people who now occupy the islands--black, brown, and white;

22

African, European, American, Spanish, French, East Indian, Chinese, Portuguese, Jew, and Dutch etc.—originally 'belonged' there. So Lamming adopts memory and imagination to revive their identity.

The Caribbean is the space where the creolizations and assimilations and syncretism were negotiated. It also has to be understood as the place of many continuous displacements. It stands for the endless ways in which Caribbean people have been destined to 'migrate'--continually between centre and periphery as the exile of Lamming. Thus, the Caribbean identity is a legacy of diaspora, of diversity, of hybridity and difference. The diaspora experience as Hall intends it here—is defined by the recognition of a necessary heterogeneity and diversity; by a conception of 'identity' which lives with and through, not despite difference, by 'hybridity'. 'Diasporic identities' are those which are constantly producing and reproducing themselves anew, through transformation and difference. One can only think here of what is uniquely—'essentially'—Caribbean: manifestly the mixes of race, ethnicity, language etc. To conclude this section with Lamming's view on the Caribbean identity, he wants to retain an autonomous identity: "I refrain from saying that I am from the West Indies, for it implies a British colonial limitation. I say rather, I am from the Caribbean" (215).

Role of History in Constructing Nationalism:

The concept of identity is entangled with the concept of nationalism that involves a sense of belonging and collectivity. And national history provides people with a sense of shared origins, a sense of common past, spirit and an identity in the present. Relevant to this issue is Michel Foucault's contention that every social discourse, which involves a politically generated truth-claim, encounters a counter-discourse that challenges the original discourse's legitimacy. In this case, power produces or creates notions of 'truth'. So, truth for Foucault often seems nothing more than the outcome of a struggle between competing discourses.

History is a form of discourse. Many scholars agree that the history of a (formerly) colonized territory is generally erased or distorted by the colonizer, replaced with the colonizer's history; and in the case of the Caribbean—"any attempt to uncover the past meant dealing not only with the noise of conflicting memories, but with silence" (Boehmer 197). Uncertainty of identity reflects their uncertainty of past. So the need to make history foreshadows Fanon's scheme of inevitable epistemic violence. Now, I would focus on how history can be constructed, deconstructed and reconstructed in the Caribbean context, as implicit in Lamming.

Colonial Construction of the Caribbean History:

History is a significant form of canonical discourse. It is defined as a record of what has happened in the past. It is also expected to be true and objective, though the limitations of our very human experience often make the quality of being true and objective impossible. In most cases, it is the dominant culture or group that writes history; as such, history is made to serve the interest of the ruling party. Following this tradition, when the European colonizers approached any country, one thing they would do in the beginning was to write the history of the colonized indigenous people.

According to the Western views, the Caribbean is a destitute nation without history and achievement. Written from Eurocentric point of view, this history is often far from reality, full of misinterpreted or distorted images of the indigenous heroes and people, in order to legitimize colonial mission and subordinating the natives. For example, the European historiographic discourses would describe the natives in the Caribbean islands as 'cannibals' only after a very vague account written by Columbus long time ago. But actually those writers never met any people who can truly be called eater of human flesh. Such myth or history in colonial countries is, therefore, nothing but a means of colonial hegemony. The colonial accounts chronicled by the colonizers are radically opposed to any impartial, adequate and accurate phenomenon of the Caribbean. And they have manipulated the Caribbean identity before the world to a great extent.

Postcolonial Reconstruction of the Caribbean History:

One of the chief tasks of the postcolonial thinkers and writers has been to rewrite history of the indigenous people and thus to restore dignity to its own identity. Derek Walcott in his influential essay "The Muse of History" criticizes those postcolonial intellectuals who angrily lament over the destruction of the historical past; he rather focuses on the possibility of a 'historyless' world which provides the Caribbean an 'Adamic' opportunity to rewrite their history afresh. Lamming's quest for identity in *The Pleasures of Exile* incorporates such a vision and mission. He has made us change our way of seeing and made us see history as the collective experience of people. For instance, he has revived the unyielding patriotic spirit of the Caribbean martyrs throughout the colonial history, whose unyielding resistance against the colonizer 'masters' is a testimony of the nation's dignified identity. In this way, history becomes active, dynamic and inspirational for their prospective decolonization, rather than a mere account of the past cause and effect.

In reference to the textual context, the Haitian "Ceremony of the souls" is Lamming's symbolic way of regenerating the Caribbean history. Here, through the ritual of calling upon spirits of the dead to speak through the living, the past is reactivated in the present. He asserts—"the symbolic function of the ceremony for me, as an artist within the Caribbean situation, is the necessity of recounting the past with each moment of conscious living". According to Supriya Nair, 'Vodum rite' here signifies a practice restricted by the colonials as a taboo; and in reanimating the dead, who speak to and through the living descendants, it revives the trial of colonial history and presents new and unusual evidence. Again, speculating about what the absent Sycorax and Miranda's unnamed mother might have told us in *The Tempest* that counter Prospero's version, Lamming says provocatively—"our knowledge must be postponed until some arrangement comparable to the Haitian Ceremony of the souls returns them to tell us what we should and ought to know [as the Caribbean]" (116). It demonstrates Lamming's counter-discursive strategy to relive the Caribbean historical identity.

Besides, Lamming's stance on the question of history is that literature itself contributes to the ambitious enterprise of the making of history. He does not always read history conventionally as significant events exclusive of everyday life; rather he considers literature to be a kind of imaginative record that paradoxically substantiates challenges and destabilizes the claims of 'rationalist' accounts in colonial historical metanarratives. He claims that the 'emergence' of the West Indian novel is the third significant historical event in the modern Caribbean, because it is most suited for representing the inner experiences of the West Indian communities and thus plays the role of "an imaginative interpretation of West Indian society by West Indians" (41). To me, as he is a part of the Caribbean literary canon, this is also a kind of self-glorification that upholds the Caribbean identity.

To Lamming, the first significant event in the Caribbean history is Columbus' entry and the second is the abolition of slavery. However, the primacy he gives Columbus does not necessarily indicate that anything before the so-called discovery of the Indies was insignificant. Rather, it emphasizes his perception of the Caribbean as repopulated and manufactured, more than any other site of imperial dominance, as first and foremost a colony, a subaltern existence that precedes all essences associated with their postcolonial identity. In this way, though he initiates with Columbus, by referring to the Caribbean literary achievement as the third important historical event, he displaces the complacency of the first. He argues that novel gives voice to the anti-colonial struggles of the Caribbean peasants, as we find in the project of Indian 'Subaltern Studies Group'; and it oversets the predicted trajectory of the dominant, i.e., Western history.

Lamming subverts the trends of the Western grand narratives by acknowledging the fundamental importance of peasant or folk life as the subject matter in any story about the Caribbean islands. Thus, he celebrates the Caribbean tradition and peasant sensibility, as a part of establishing their identity. His conviction is that agricultural past is the common background-umbrella under which a national Caribbean identity can be re-constructed. And taking raw materials from this proletarian class for his writing, a Caribbean writer can truly write back and disempower to the metropolitan centre. Otherwise, his identity would be annihilated from himself and the world. Hereby, Lamming tries to outline what Gordon Rohlehr sees as a nascent theory about the relation of West Indian writers to their roots. So the past is crucial to his present identity.

27

"Caliban Orders History" can be called a classic example of Lamming's counter-discursive essays. Here he extends a literary character to fit the "unforgotten and unforgettable" (150) historical figure Toussaint L'Ouverture, one of the leaders of the Haitian Revolution in 1791 and the primary figure in James's *Black Jacobins*. The theme of it is the transformation of slaves trembling before a white man into people being able to organize themselves and defeat the most powerful European nations of their day. Lamming regards it as a great epic of revolutionary struggle and achievement too. To adjoin my focal point in this regard, the novel can be called a historiographic metafiction on the Caribbean identity.

Lamming states that James "shows us Caliban as Prospero had never known him; a slave who was a great soldier in battle, an incomparable administrator in public affairs; full of paradox but never without compassion, a humane leader of men" (119). He is, of course, thinking of the invertion of power-play between the slaves and the masters, and in his own context the image applies to the peasants as well. The historical persona of Toussaint reinvents the stereotypical savage Caliban in Shakespeare's *The Tempest*, rendering a familiar interpretation of the play suspect by transferring the possibilities of the Haitian Revolution into the realm of fictional drama. But by making so intimate an incorporation of history into literature, Lamming also disrupts the scientific or factual claims of history, a disruption that is shared by James's polemical confrontation with the imperial version of the Haitian Revolution that dismissed the troublesome, former slave, Toussaint. His 'revisionist' tendency in respect of the Caribbean historical identity matches with N'gugi's opinion in *Petals of Blood*: 'To understand the present … you must understand the past'. Indeed, the past humanizes Lamming's African legacy.

To conclude this section, how history might be 'rewritten'--is a crucial question for the self-representation of colonized people. And postcolonial approach has changed the ways people would approach the problems of history, identity, race, place and displacement. Colonizer's version of history about the Caribbean is subverted symbolically and Lamming as a native is writing his own history. He re-visits and rewrites the Caribbean history to revive the truth and make his nation aware as a necessity for attaining the freedom from the body and mind forged manacles of the Empire. Through history he wants to unify the Caribbean: " … what could hold Indians and Negroes together in Trinidad … is their common background of social history which can be called West Indian … whose basic feature is the peasant sensibility" (224-25). Nationalism becomes his way of transcending colonial history in his quest for self-definition or identity. Throughout his extended dialogue with James's *The Black Jacobins*, Lamming's persona identifies him with a tradition of resistance and lays claim to the Haitian heroic revolution as a facet of his New-World-Caribbean identity on behalf of the whole Caribbean. Thus, the Caribbean history is a history of foreign aggressions and native resistance. And, it seems to be his exposition of the responsibility of intellectual engagement with the colonial situation. In my chapter on postcolonial interpretation of *The Tempest*, I would illustrate Lamming's revisioning the Caribbean history more.

Chapter III

Representation of the Caribbean in Colonial-Discourses:

The Caribbean is a neglected and often misrepresented area of the world. According to Homi K. Bhabha, "colonialism and postcolonialism are very much about identities and the ways these are constructed and deconstructed by discourses ... The address to nation as narration stresses the insistence of political power and cultural authority". And practically, colonial-discourses are established by and for the colonizers as the instruments of power and subject-formation. It implies a process of judgment and discrimination, and has an unspoken authority. In Bhabha's words, the objective of colonial-discourse is to interpret the colonized as a population of degenerate types on the basis of racial origin in order to justify conquest and to establish systems of administration and instruction. At the same time, he observes that postcolonial migrant people can destabilize traditional identities and violate supposedly mutually exclusive categories because they are simultaneously of both the East and the West.

Discourse produces a subject dependent upon the rules of the system of knowledge that produces it. And discourses are always, to Foucault, a function of the power of those who control the discourse to determine knowledge. Politics of representation is much integrated with discourse and postcolonial identity. In Ashcroft's words, European texts—anthropology, history, drama, fiction etc. captured the non-European subject within European frameworks that read his or her alterity as 'terror' or 'lack'. Such texts—the representations of Europe to itself, and the representation of others to Europe—were not accounts of different peoples and societies, but a projection of European fears and desires masquerading as scientific/'objective' knowledge.

To conclude, in the Caribbean context the colonized subject has been characterized through colonial discourses as 'other', 'primitive' and 'cannibal'--as a means of establishing the 'binary' separation of the colonizer and colonized, and asserting the naturalness and primacy of the colonizing culture and world view. It is through, in Althusser's term of the 'Ideological State Apparatuses', education system and in terms of modes of production and consumption like the services of BBC, popular television shows, cartoons etc. through which colonialist representations persist and currently circulate, and thus construct the Caribbean identity. Thus, a discursive practice, according to Foucault, 'controls the dissemination of certain knowledge, thereby ensuring the domination of certain social interests by producing a certain kind of subject'.

Politics of Modern Western Media:

Western Media have played a vital role in constructing the black Afro-Caribbean's identity as 'savage' other and sustaining the imperialist purposes. For instance, when an African appears on media screen, the focus is concentrated on his craziness to prove the African's mythologized identity. Besides, his curly hair is presented as a symbol of savagery. Meanwhile, Lamming became a broadcaster for the BBC Colonial service 'Caribbean Voices' in 1951, actually to figure out the root of the problems of colonization like—*why do these white people think themselves to be so superior that they can dominate and colonize any other?* (Italics Mine). However, the programme (1945-58) was the first serious acknowledgement in a metropolitan country, of the existence and importance of a corpus of Anglophone writing in the Caribbean and of a group of writers, many unknown to each other, seriously working in that area. Moreover, in an interview taken at the East Coast of Barbados in 1989, Lamming said:

> I worked for a number of years with the BBC ... Caribbean Voices ... I came to realise that over the years, that there was a Caribbean reality which was there, which touched different territories in different ways, but which had not yet come fully into the consciousness of each territory ... So the evolution of each territory depends very much on the forging and the incorporating of that Caribbean reality into the consciousness of each.

However, though the media nurtured the Caribbean's sense of identity, the politics of representation and negative identity-construction worked behind it.

In "Introduction" to *The Pleasures of Exile,* Lamming has dismantled that the main purpose of the BBC was not only to broadcast the Caribbean news, but also to show the world a tribal ritual of the natives named 'Vodum rites'. As he clarifies this cultural identity—

> This ceremony of the souls is regarded by the Haitian peasant as a solemn communion; for he hears, at first hand, the secrets of the Dead. The celebrants are mainly relatives of the deceased who, ever since their death, have been locked in Water. It is duty of the Dead to

32

return and offer, on this momentous night, a full and honest report on their past relations with the living … The living demand to hear whether there is any need for forgiveness, for redemption; whether, in fact, there may be any guide which may help them towards reforming their present condition. (9-10)

Actually, the purpose of the BBC was to address the world that—*Look at these Caribbean people! They have such customs and rituals. Look at the difference. We are so enlightened and civilized; while they are still down to earth and superstitious people. That is why we feel that it has been our humanitarian duty to civilize them by colonial mission for centuries* (Italics Mine). Again, it seems to me that Lamming has 'depoliticized' the politics inherent in the broadcasting of such an indigenous culture. That is, he might have warned the contemporary nation that as the Caribbean, they could not be free unless they had come to terms with a past like the Haitian 'Vodum rite' or the Ceremony of the Souls.

However, out of self-justifying conviction, Western media and languages have been used as tools for colonization. Just as the dead are coming back by the 'magic box' radio, Prospero, the colonizer, becomes resurrected. I would explain Prospero/Caliban metaphor in the formation of the Caribbean identity in my discussion on *The Tempest*. My point here is that Lamming challenges the criteria of identity that the British colonizers have imposed on the colonized natives, and their worldwide propaganda through the media to justify that the colonizers are a form of 'Saviour' for these 'uncivilized' Caribbean. Indeed, it is their hegemonic attitude.

Representation of the Caribbean's ancestors through popular culture is another tool for identity formation. In "The African Presence", Lamming discovers that the Africans' appearance in the Western films functions as an Ideological State Apparatus too:

They are arranged like nature in scenes which are to suggest the authenticity of a native crowd in the background. In moments of tension, they may be asked to stand still: statues of mourning [no expression] … Sometimes these Africans are asked to shout at a retreating white pirate who argues that he didn't mean to shoot the elephant. (165)

In such representation, the curiosity of the spectators would be to know what words the Africans actually shout in that dark forest. But the media is unable to decipher the meaning. So the media have no right to propagate that the European colonizers enlightened the Africans with their language. Again, in some films "the African appears as Butlers. Like a privileged slave who shows signs of learning…" He "speaks only with hands. He hears his name take the form of salt, butter, or bread; and he answers with some receptacle containing food" (165). To cite Althusser here, it seems to me that metaphorically he is interpellated into something that can fulfill the European's colonial appetite. He only knows how to obey the white masters perfectly—before having a sense of self-existence and identity as a human being. The film conditions the psyche of young Africans in such a way that later "they discuss and dramatize the contents of their memory" (165). Since the plot represents the African as barbarous and the Western stranger as 'the great saviour', unconsciously they believe, internalize and accept their subjectivity constructed by audio-visual discourse. Here lies the politics of pleasure. Again, idea of mimicry is apparent in Lamming's indication of "the false laugh which the West Indian summons as he watches the film brutalization of the African's personality in the role of a moon-cow" (181).

The impact of the Western narrative cinema in the lives of the young Africans is that they cannot distinguish between phantasy world and the real world. For instance, unemployment problem compels them to lead a life as represented in the cinematic world from where they want to get everything they like. The result of such identification is often disillusionment, despair or distress. Sometimes it demands their imprisonment and they cannot explain the reasons of their subversion before the court. Their dumbness is taken as stupidity; and they have to depend on justice of Heaven or power of magic because law is blind. But none understands that this speechlessness is the whole predicament of black slaves. In a word, the aggression of media-politics worked and is still working subtly and steadily to represent the black Africans as 'savages' and devil-like, to justify the colonial 'civilizing mission'.

34

In response, post-colonial resistance to such representations has taken many forms; e.g., the widespread contemporary practice of counter-canonical literary discourse, as discussed by Helen Tiffin. Processes of artistic and literary decolonization have involved a radical dis/mantling of European codes and a post-colonial subversion and appropriation of the dominant European discourses. This has frequently been accompanied by the demand for an entirely new or wholly recovered 'reality', free of all colonial taint. Given the nature of the relationship between colonizers and colonized in the Caribbean context, with its pandemic brutalities and its cultural denigration, such a demand is desirable and inevitable.

Early Images of the Caribbean in Canonical Discourses

The Caribbean identity rooted with Africa is based on myths found in dominant discourses. The Caribbean has held a significant place in European literature and voyage-narratives from the sixteenth century onwards. Images on those writing have exerted a powerful influence on thinking about the Caribbean and the nature of colonization there. As Lamming has found that such writing has constituted a trend of canon, he feels committed to reinterpret, reject or rewrite some of those myths from a Caribbean perspective. In "Introduction" of *The Pleasures of Exile*, Lamming scrutinizes the Caribbean mythologized identity as 'cannibals' in the first voyage-narrative of an English knight Sir John Haukins in October 1562, which documents—"The Canybals of that Island … are the most desperate warriers that are in the Indies, by the Spaniardes report, who are never able to conquer them … they were driven ashore, and so taken by them [the Carib Indian], and eaten" (13). Thus a seed of colonization is subtly and richly infused with mythologized identity of the Caribbean as 'savages'. And the myth of England's supremacy in taste and judgment begins in a West Indian from the earliest stages of his education. To Lamming, such a "myth is most difficult to dislodge" (26).

In "The Occasion for Speaking" too, Lamming has quoted the great German philosopher Hegel's last word on Africa in his Introduction to *The Philosophy of History*:

> Africa proper, as far as History goes back, has remained—for all purposes of connection with the rest of the world—shut up; it is the Gold-land [which might have allured colonizers] compressed within itself--the land of childhood, which lying beyond the days of self-conscious history, is enveloped in the dark mantle of Night … it is no historical part of the world; it has no movement or development to exhibit … still involved in the *conditions of mere nature…* (32)

Then Lamming evaluates this canonical discourse by stating—"what disqualifies African man from Hegel's world of History is his apparent incapacity to evolve with the logic of language which is the only aid man has in capturing the Idea. African man, for Hegel, has no part in the common pursuit of the Universal" (32). Lamming also indicates that it is the colonizing pressure of the European claim which creates an element of embarrassment in the American Negro Baldwin's glance towards Africa:

'… a vision of the bush, primitive, night-black in its inaccessibility' [as Conrad's *The Heart of Darkness*] … We know what is meant by bush. It is the tom-tom and the axe: the tom-tom always loud with noise, and the axe for ever suggestive of blood. It is here, perhaps, that the old white myth and fear of superb sexual potency in the black male may have started. (33)

Thus, the African are thought and taken into consideration through rumour and myth, by the foreign tutelage growing a sense of fear about Africa as a world beyond human intervention. In postcolonial criticism, 'myth' can be said to imply a romanticized, distorted or false set of attitudes; and is therefore close to the sense of 'stereotype'. And the Western discourses have constructed negative myths on the origin of the black Caribbean—which Lamming tries to deconstruct counter-discursively for reconstructing the reality of the Caribbean identity.

Interesting but significant for the Caribbean identity, in "A Way of seeing", Lamming discusses about an American novelist whose some books have been "set in the West Indies … But she had never seen the Caribbean. She recreated the atmosphere from general reading". Lamming wonders whether it is "the indirect colonial influence of *The Tempest*" (71). This is a remarkable instance of the formation and dissemination of stereotype Caribbean identity by armchair discourses. In Sylvia Wynter's view, it is the *myth* of Europe which rejects all other experiences, African, Indian, Chinese etc. which contribute to the being of the West Indian.

Again, the impact of colonial discourse on a West Indian Negro is expressed in "The African Presence". Lamming says that such a person's relation to Africa is "problematic" because--

He knows it through rumour and myth which is made sinister by a foreign tutelage, and he becomes, through the gradual conditioning of his education, identified with fear: fear of that continent as a world beyond human intervention. Part product of that world, and living still under the shadow of its past disfigurement, he appears reluctant to acknowledge his share of

the legacy which is part of his heritage. (160-161)

Ideological Resistance to Mythologized Representations:

There is a proverb: 'Tit for tat'. So, where there is colonial representation and ideological conditioning, there must be some sort of resistance—of which Lamming's *The Pleasures of Exile* is a classic example. Its counter-discursive essays challenge both the values and beliefs that colonizers have imposed on the native populations, and the assumption that European colonization is superior and bring civilization to indigenous cultures. From Said's perspective, it can be called an "ideological resistance"; because the declining state of the Western hegemony during 1950s opened up space for the writers' effort to restore back the lost sense of a unity to the contemporary disintegrated Caribbean communities which were still under the British colonial system. To cite Lemert's view in this point: the destabilizing of the modern world is associated with a curious, but undeniable energizing of identity as the topic of widespread political interest.

Put simply, canonical counter-discourse destabilizes the power/knowledge axis of imperialism. There are many counter-discursive possibilities even within one culture's encounter with the master narratives which have impacted upon its history. In the next chapter, I would like to establish that Lamming's route of subverting Shakespearean canon *The Tempest* is an ideological attempt to renegotiate the Caribbean identity allegorically.

Chapter IV

Deconstruction of Canonical Discourse *The Tempest* & Reconstruction of the Caribbean Allegorical Identity:

The ugly incident of colonialism in the Caribbean islands has effects on language, education, religion, artistic sensibilities, popular culture and the like. Regarding education, Lamming makes explicit in "The Occasion for speaking" his perception of the colonial education system as a means of ideological control which suffocated any expression of a Caribbean consciousness. Post-colonial critical writings in the region have therefore become veritable weapons used to dismantle the hegemonic boundaries/forces and the determinants that create unequal relations of power, based on binary oppositions. Therefore, it is true to say that the primary concern of most post-colonial Caribbean literature is to salvage the history of their people that colonialism has taken off or manipulated. Lamming responds to the urgency and inevitability of this historic mission. He has selected a canonical drama as his counter-discursive resistance or intervention. Some essays in *The Pleasures of Exile* draw parallelism and shows paradox between the characters in *The Tempest* and the Caribbean slave situations; figure out racial binaries and the threat of miscegenation, represent the New World 'other' as opposed to the European 'self', troped as a form of the nature/culture dichotomy; and interest in power relationship involving dominance, subservience, and rebellion. In this section, I would like to express that what is primary on his mind and central to his subversion and allegorical deconstruction of this English canon--is the urge to put the record straight and illuminate the threshold between past and present, thought and action, self and other, and the Caribbean and the world. In other words, his essays provide the answers to the questions of how the British colonizers became successful to fall apart the things related to the Caribbean identity.

Shakespeare: A Legacy of Colonization

In "The Occasion for Speaking", Lamming makes explicit his perception of the colonial education system as a means of ideological control which suffocated any expression of a Caribbean consciousness. The objection points to the Eurocentric saturation of literary consciousness. Again, the cultural politics of the canon and the way in which the now familiar notion of the English literature was constructed in line with the colonial project to educate the natives, has generated interesting debates within the Caribbean literature as a foreshadow of their counter-discourse. For instance, the circulation of "Shakespeare's Books" within [the Caribbean] educational and cultural spheres has been a powerful hegemonic force throughout the history of the British Empire.[1] In can be called an 'epistemic violence' in Foucault's term. Nevertheless, *The Tempest* remains the text most widely chosen for counter-discursive interrogations of the Shakespearean canon. Paul Brown points out that it can be reread as not simply a reflection of colonialist practices but an intervention in an ambivalent and even contradictory discourse. Lamming's re-reading of the play provides a critical insight into the political relationship between the Caribbean and the European. A rebellious island native Caliban is enslaved by a colonizing Milanese Duke Prospero in *The Tempest,* and has become a favourite symbol of revolutionary, anti-imperialist culture for the Caribbean writers, especially since 1950s. Lamming himself clarifies his intention "to make use of *The Tempest* as a way of presenting a certain state of feeling which is the heritage of the exiled and colonial writer from the British Caribbean" (9). He also sees "*The Tempest* against the background of England's experimentation in colonization … *The Tempest* was also prophetic of a political future which is our present. Moreover, the circumstances of my life, both as a colonial and exiled descendant of Caliban in the twentieth century, is an example of that prophecy" (13).

Now, in our awareness of the destructiveness of Western colonialism, we should return to ideas that were commonplace in the sixteenth century. Reports from the New World differed widely in their descriptions of the Indians; to some they were demons or savage beasts, to others they were unfallen men. As post-colonial critics often imply, the name *Caliban* is an anagram of *Cannibal*, a word

41

introduced to England shortly after Columbus dubbed the natives to the West Indies *canibales*, mishearing the name *Caribs*, and saddled them with a reputation for eating human flesh. In *The Tempest* Caliban is similarly characterized as a half-human, half-monster. In opposition, Prospero casts the role of imperial and civilizing force. And both have been a metaphor in postcolonial literature for many years. That is why, Lamming metonymies the Caribbean with Caliban and the British Empire with Prospero. Hence, the conflict between Prospero as the colonizer and Caliban as the colonized becomes paradigmatic of the major historical opposition and the overarching dialectic of the Caribbean colonies.

It is on the basis of the foregoing background that in this section, I propose to examine how Lamming uses his essays to facilitate the transgression of boundaries and subversion of hegemonic rigidities previously mapped out in precursor canonical literary texts about the Caribbean and her people. A canon is a set of reading practices. And the subversion of a canon involves not simply the bringing to consciousness of these practices, or the deployment of some hierarchy of value within them; but equally crucially the reconstruction of the so-called canonical texts through alternative reading practices. Since Shakespeare is representative enough in the canon of colonialist discourse, Lamming has re-written his play *The Tempest* allegorically long before Derrida's theory of Deconstruction, and from a postcolonial perspective. By allegory, I refer not only to an extended metaphor or symbolic reference observed by a critic from outside the work, but also the structural principle of the work itself. In *The Pleasures of Exile* he attempts to engage in dialectical intertextuality with this long existing canonical work that metaphorically presents the negative stereotypes of the Caribbean, e.g., by attributing bestiality, deformity, lust, ugliness and degeneracy with Caliban. The chapter also seeks to consider how counter-canonical literature provides an avenue for the Caribbean writers to represent not only 'Self' but also their European 'Other'.

Lamming's *The Pleasures of Exile* is an elaborate recasting of William Shakespeare's play, not only employing the island worlds of that work as symbols for aspects of Caribbean experience but also commenting upon its role as a text that had contributed to the British colonial mindset. Here he examines the Caribbean colonial past, decolonization, and his own identity. According to his postcolonial reading, the crew's suffering in the sea due to the tempest created by Prospero allegorically refers to the horrible situation of the slaves transported from Africa through the middle Passage to the Caribbean plantation. Lamming identifies himself with Caliban, Prospero's slave on a remote island where Caliban is tortured for servitude, like the Caribbean slaves who would be tortured savagely by their colonial masters. He parallels Prospero's imprisonment of Caliban in the rock with the colonizer's emergency regulations against the native sons who were not allowed to travel certain Caribbean orbit "marked out and even made legal by a foreign visitor" (102). His slave imagery can largely be justified with a New Historicist reading of even an English discourse *Oroonoko* set in that New World. However, he reflects the Caribbean slaves' asserting rebellious and courageous spirit against their masters, which upholds their individuality and identity.

Again, in Lamming's deconstructive reading, Ariel, Prospero's source of information, represents the unspeakable secret police or spy in the context of the Caribbean colonies. To make Ariel aware of his inferiority, the 'benevolent' Prospero constantly reminds him how he saved him from Sycorax's torture. Similarly the Caribbean slaves were constantly reminded what a great 'saviour' the European were, who saved these deformed savages from further sin by Christening or baptizing them, though they must suffer in this world for expiation. They were conditioned to believe that God was punishing them because they were 'ignorant'; at the same time, God's most 'favourite' children on earth. Thus the colonizers in this domain also politicized religion.

Meanwhile, Prospero had originally behaved towards Caliban with a show of 'human care' and 'nurture', but with the same assumption of superiority which had been rationalized as benevolence by the colonists in the New World, who, calling the native Africans 'savages'--because their religion was not Christianity, their civilization unlike European civilization, their language not English or Spanish, their countenance and cultures outlandish--denied them full humanity and any freedom even to their own lands, and exported them firstly to England, dead or alive, to be exhibited at fairs; and later to the

43

Caribbean plantations as slaves. The possibility was debated that they might not be human at all, but humanoid monsters created as slaves for humanity.

Again, Lamming dismantles the hierarchy of Prospero, Ariel and Caliban. Caliban is no longer seen as the creature outside civilization "on whose nature/ Nurture can never stick" (*Tempest* IV. i. 188-9), but as a human being (specifically a West Indian) whose human status is denied by the European claims to an exclusive human condition. In traditional reading, Caliban is seen not simply as an American Indian. He is also very much in the tradition of the *wodwo*, or wild man of the woods, so familiar in English art and folklore of the thirteenth and fourteenth centuries. But in his 'Introduction to 1984 edition', Lamming counters that if Prospero could be seen as the symbol of the European imperial enterprise, then Caliban should be embraced as the continuing possibility of a profound revolutionary change initiated by Toussaint L'Ouverture in the Haitian war of independence. He also states metaphorically that the Cuban revolution was a Caribbean response to that imperial menace which Prospero conceived as a 'civilising mission'. Thus he re-reads the canonical and colonial discourse from the perspective of Caliban or the Caribbean. Supriya Nair in *Caliban's Curse* argues that Lamming's work expands the protest of Shakespeare's Caliban to articulate a reinvention of the Caribbean cultures.

Regarding Prospero's gaze and Caliban's identity, Lamming's essay "In the Beginning" discovers the latter as only a languageless and inarticulate savage in *The Tempest*. Again, Stephano recognizes Caliban, as we go through the essay "A Monster, A Child, A Slave": "This is some monster of the isle with four legs … If I can recover him, and keep him tame, and get to Naples with him, he's a present for any emperor…" (108). As we know--the colonial explorers' hegemonic ideology led them to interpellate the African's identity as an exotic other, fascinating enough for exhibition in European markets—is apparent here. In Miranda's subconscious view as well, Caliban is seen "as the descendant of a Devil" (111).

From Foucault's perspective, Prospero takes control over Caliban and his Island through the "absolute wisdom" (22) and magical power. As a result, Caliban becomes an 'other' in his own island

and is treated brutally like the Caribbean slaves by Prospero's magic rod. But he does not kill this beast. The reason behind this may be that if he kills Caliban, he will lose "his source of food" (99), and his authority because there will be no one upon whom he can exert his authority and power. Hegel's master/slave dialectical idea is explicit in Lamming's reading.

In his re-reading of this English classic as a political allegory, Lamming concentrates on the issue of 'good government' in the island and extends it to encompass his sense of the injustice of Prospero's dispossession of Caliban's inheritance—

> I must eat my dinner.
>
> This island's mine, by Sycorax my mother,
>
> Which thou tak'st from me When thou cam'st first,
>
> Thou strok'st me …
>
> … keep from me
>
> The rest o' th' island. (*Tempest*, I .i.)

We can sense that Prospero's trick to give Caliban his supper sometimes only to ensure that he would not revolt, has a metaphorical resemblance with the relationship between the European colonial masters and the Caribbean colonized slaves. Lamming also identifies Ariel and Caliban as "the two agents of labour and public relations without whom he would be helpless" (114), as Hegel observes. What Lamming implies but does not say is that the allegory manifests the strategy learned by Shakespeare's Empire to apply on the Caribbean.

To repeat Foucault, our identity is constructed by the way we are seen through the dominant gaze. In *The Tempest* Prospero's gaze fixes the identity and status of Caliban but not vice versa, as Lamming looks back in anger to discover that--

Caliban is never accorded the power *to see*. He is always the measure of the condition which his physical appearance has already defined. Caliban is … eternally below possibility … He is seen as … a state of existence [as though ordained by 'original Law', as Lamming says at page 110], which can be appropriated and exploited for the purposes of another's own development. Caliban is a reminder of … the evil vigour of the Beast that is always there … his skin is black … the colour of his loss and the absence of any soul. (107-8)

In reality, construction of such an identity perpetuated the slave exploitation in the Caribbean sugar plantations throughout the colonial era.

Now, mistress-slave dialectical relationship in the Caribbean context is expanded as a central part in Lamming's metaphorical interpretation. Caliban and the child Miranda are assumed by Lamming to have grown closer by the necessary contact of servant and mistress. Caliban might have had to carry Miranda on his back and play with her, the way the Caribbean have seen African servants showing their affection to the European (masters') children. In return, she "taught thee each hour/One thing or other … I endow'd thy purposes/With words that made them known" (*Exile*, 109). It is as if her Eurocentric knowledge is the standard and any African lacking it is identified as ignorant, uncivilized etc.

Religious discourse also has a major bearing on the Caribbean colonization and identity formation. As Lamming finds,

Education, meaning the possession of the Word—which was in the beginning or not at all—is the tool which Prospero has tried on the irredeemable nature of his savage and deformed slave … Only the application of the Word to the darkness of Caliban's world could harness the beast which resides within this cannibal. This is the most important achievement of the colonizing process. (109)

To me, firstly the emphasis on Word conforms to the structuralist linguist Claude Levi Strauss and the psychoanalytic critic Jacques Lacan's view in the sense that—words constitute our world (with ideas).

46

As we find here, Prospero's words constitute Caliban's and Miranda's world and identity, the way the colonizer's words/ideas constituted that of the Caribbean. That is why Lamming comes forward to deconstruct them. Secondly, it is often said that--to name something with words is to give it identity and possess it. The example is apparent in Lamming's citing Caliban's protest against Prospero— "When thou cam'st first, thou ... teach me how to name the bigger light...' (Lamming 101). Thirdly, Lamming's use of the capitalized form of the 'Word' may refer to the Bible or manipulation of Christianity over the Caribbean religion.

The colonizers thus mutually exploited race and religion, as Lamming remarks ironically about a Christian vision: "The African [many Caribbean's ancestors] did not achieve the word because he acquired a phenomenal aptitude for wickedness. God separated him from the Word so that he might sojourn in a state of illiteracy ... be punished by the greed, the deception, the cruelties of literate men [colonizers]" (86). That is why, according to colonial discourse, Lord has sent the European to enlighten them from sin and darkness. Lamming ironically calls it England's "divine right to organize the native's reading" (27) and metaphorically dismantles the issue when he ironically comments that it is some original "Law which has ordained the state of existence we call Caliban" and he is superfluous "until Prospero arrives with the aid of the Word which might help him to clarify the chaos which shows its true colours all over his skin" (110-111).

Lamming's counter-canonical-discourse continues as he announces—"This [Caribbean] island belongs to Caliban whom he [Prospero] found there; yet some privilege allows Prospero [signifying British Empire] to assert--with an authority that is divine—that he is lord of the island" (113). Next we come across Prospero's "divine hierarchy of which he is the most privileged on earth!" (116). Lamming ends the chapter with the question: "Will the Lie upon which Prospero's confident authority was built be discovered?" (117). In reality, it is Lamming's commitment as a spokesman of the Caribbean to decolonize their (Blakean) 'mind-forged manacles' and convey the Truth.

Lamming's counter-discourse further suggests that the people of the colonized country like the Caribbean are exiled from their root (by the uprooting process of the colonizers), from their history (as history was first written by the colonizers), from their native language (as they had to use the masters' languages for communication), from their native culture and religion (as they had felt a sense of inferiority for their own culture and rituals). To him, Caliban is colonized by language and excluded by language. He is exiled from his gods, his nature and his own name—all related to his identity. Thus the colonized people all over the world are exiled whether living in their own country or in the metropolitan culture for being the refugee; and for the Caribbean, it creates a sense of identity crisis. Reading Lamming's re-reading the textual conscious and unconscious of *The Tempest*, I would like to assert my hypothesis that Shakespeare is a legacy of the British Empire in the Caribbean context.

English Language as a Colonizing and Decolonizing Weapon

To some postcolonial critics, the politics of language is integrated with the issue of identity. Towards the end, Lamming's subversion of the English canon shows the duplicity and hypocrisy by which Prospero's dispossession is effected and stress is laid on the eagerness and willingness with which Caliban initially offers to share the fruits of the island with the shipwrecked Prospero and his child. Prospero's assertion that in exchange he has given Caliban the gift of language—is undercut in Lamming's reading by this fact of material dispossession, and thus Lamming asserts the injustice through Caliban's response: "and my profit on't/Is, I know how to curse" (*The* Tempest, I.ii.425-6). Lamming goes on to suggest that language is not simply a gift and a curse to be used--in the dialogue between Prospero and Caliban, besides "not to curse our meeting-but to push it further, reminding the descendants of both sides that what's done is done, and can only be seen as a soil from which other gifts, or the same gift endowed with different meanings, may grow towards a future which is colonized by our acts in this moment, but which must always remain open". This dialectic of domination and resistance is central to Lamming's approaches to language. He allows the voices of Caliban and the noises of Prospero's isle to articulate the promises of decolonization.

Again, language is a part and parcel of the Caribbean identity. As Firdous Azim says, "Identity of a postcolonial writer is established by the colonizer's language; and this relationship has the bearing on the emerging sense of nationhood". In elaboration, the kind of language used by a writer may reflect what kind of community s/he is from, what kind of community s/he wants to identify with, even what kind of audience s/he wants to speak to or write for. After Lamming's exile to the metropolis of London, he claims: "I am a direct descendant of slaves, too near to the actual enterprise to believe that its echoes are over with the reign of emancipation. Moreover, I am a direct descendant of Prospero worshipping in the same temple of endeavour, using his legacy of language…."

On the one hand, Lamming is a descendant of Caliban who has lost his motherland and mother tongue. In his view, language is the speech, concept, method and of course, the way of creating self identity. In that sense, language is the prison for Caliban because he can only think of going to a

49

certain point, but not beyond. To look back through *The Empire Writes Back*, slaves for the Caribbean plantations were isolated (where possible) from their common language group and transported and sold in "mixed lots", as a deliberate means of limiting the possibilities of rebellion. Further, Lamming has related the colonizers' imposition of language with that of Law and believes that "it is language in this sense which enables Prospero to climb to his throne" (157) and abuse his power. The result was that within one to three generations the only available tongue to the Africans for communication either among themselves or with the master was the European language of that master. This loss of their own 'voice' created a sense of their alienation and identity crisis.

On the other hand, Lamming is a descendant of Prospero by manipulating the language of the British because now he can disclose the politics of the colonizers more widely and effectively in English, like Achebe. In other words, by using, wielding, bending and abrogating the English language, he conveys and upholds the Caribbean realities and experiences. He even goes to the extent of saying that "what the West Indians do with it [English language] is their own business" (36). He celebrates the West Indian novelists' identity by reasserting that they have "contributed to English reading" (44) by writing in English. Ultimately, he has been able to contribute to the elaboration of his national consciousness before the international readers and thus reconstruct the Caribbean identity.

Again, language, for Fanon, is weighted with historical and dialectical tensions that are grounded in the contingencies of power relations and in the existential, material, and psychological underpinnings of racism and colonialism. Speech, for Fanon, implies the relational nature of utterance—"to speak is to exist absolutely for the other … To speak means to be in a position to use certain syntax, to grasp the morphology of this or that language, but it means above all to assume a culture, to support the weight of a civilization". Language is thus a metonym for culture, and Fanon repeats this proposition in a series of rhetorical gestures that position utterance, culture, and colonization within the orbit of subject formation and colonial identity. In "A Monster, A Child, A Slave" too, Lamming asserts—

This [decolonizing] gift of language is the deepest and most delicate bond of involvement … Prospero has given Caliban language; and with it an unstated history of consequences, an unknown history of future [Lamming's present] intentions … as a way, a method, a necessary avenue towards areas of the self [Caribbean identity] which could not be reached in any other way … which makes Caliban [Caribbean writers] aware of possibilities. (109)

Again, in "A Way of Seeing", when Lamming is asserting his West Indian literary caliber in the Institute of Contemporary Arts in England in 1950, he proves that "Caliban had got hold of Prospero's weapons and decided that he would never again seek his master's permission" (63). Lamming as a creator of counter-discourse further claims—

Caliban is no longer nervous … His wish [is] to change the shape of the throne … He tells himself that Prospero doesn't really want the change to come about … He is a child of the backward glance with recollection of a time when he was not even accorded the right to be angry. He has known what it means to have one's past appropriated, then languageless as his aboriginal neighbours. (84-85)

He concludes the chapter with visionary statement that "Prospero's role is now completely reversed" (85) and Caliban is empowered against the extraterrestrial masters. Thus, the binary power-play between the British colonizers and the colonized West Indian has been deconstructed and reconstructed by Lamming's counter-discursive allegory. From racial perspective, the white literature that has been significant since the colonial exploration--is echoed, reinterpreted and appropriated as part of a growing assertion of a black-Caribbean-critical identity.

Interpolation is a crucial phenomenon in Lamming's counter-discursive mission. For instance, by interposing, intervening, and interjecting the 'dominant discourse' and giving a voice of protest to the subaltern Caliban, Lamming has 'interpolated' the influential English discourse—which Ashcroft calls "the initial and essential movement in the process of post-colonial transformation"[3]. Again, Edward Said has an evocative term for this process which he calls "the voyage in"; that is, the conscious effort of peoples from colonized countries to "enter into the discourse of Europe and the West, to mix with it, transform it, to make it acknowledge marginalized or suppressed or forgotten histories" (*Culture and Imperialism*, 261). Actually, claiming that "English is a West Indian language", Lamming takes the language as a decolonizing weapon. He resembles Caliban who is at liberty to interpret and use Prospero's language in his way of resistance.

Selwyn Cudjoe also gives a very clear account of the adaption of the master's language as an acquisition of cultural capital: "The ability to 'speak properly' and to manipulate language has always been of enormous importance to Trinidadians and Tobagonians". Lamming uses English as a cultural vehicle of resisting colonialism, a medium through which a world audience could be introduced to the features of culturally diverse Caribbean communities. But ironically, when Lamming asserts that "English is a West Indian language", he seems to acknowledge a legacy of the British Empire.

Prospero's enslavement of Caliban was established as a key paradigm in colonialist discourse. Hence, the paradigmatic importance of Lamming's revisionist reading of *The Tempest* derives from the self-conscious exploration of the filial relationship between European canonical discourses and the construction of Caribbean subjects as well as the subversive potential of the reading. He has explored the dialectical nature of their master/slave relationship, arguing for a more interactive model of colonial power structures.

By politicized reading and rewriting the characters, the narrative and the context of *The Tempest* as a counter-discourse, Lamming anticipates the post-colonial critic's preoccupation with place and displacement, racism, stereotype representation, hegemony, language, abrogation and appropriation as strategies of cultural decolonization and national reconstruction. He tends to suggest that subversion lies in Caliban's abrogation and appropriation of Prospero's language, and the destruction of a binary system of logic in which black is defined by white. He uses the postcolonial interpretation of the play also as the frame within which the themes like colonization, politics of religion, hypocrisy of the whites, capitalism, hybridity, and the Caribbean identity crisis—are injected. He himself says, "it contains and crystallizes all the conflicts which have gone before" (95). This provides him not only an archetypal metaphor for colonialism and slavery, but also an allegorical way of reversing the roles and restructuring--rather than simply rejecting--the 'realities' shared by the colonizer and colonized: "The world from which our reciprocal ways of seeing have sprung was once Prospero's world. It is no longer his. Moreover, it will never be his. It is ours, the legacy of many centuries, demanding of us a new kind of effort, a new kind of sight for viewing the possible horizons of our own century" (203). Thus it provides a means of interrogating the cultural legacy of imperialism, and offers renewed opportunities for performative intervention. Supriya Nair argues that Lamming's subversion, as a political struggle, expands the protest of Shakespeare's Caliban to articulate a reinvention of the Caribbean cultures and identity. Indeed, his deconstruction provides impetus in the resistance to Prospero or colonizer's fraudulent power and regenerates the Caribbean identity.

Chapter V

Lamming's Quest for Contemporary Caribbean Identity:

The quest for identity is one of the most important factors in the life of an individual as well as that of a nation. V.S. Naipaul says that the West Indian needs writers to tell him who he is, where he stands. Indeed, the subject of Caribbean definition has occupied and engaged almost every writer of the Caribbean region. This is natural because in so many respects writing is a form of self-definition within a certain defined society and culture. Writers write from experiences within particular societies, and their work necessarily defines both the experience and the society. Lamming has tried to define the Caribbean identity with its diverse features. So, he was influenced by the decolonizing-spirit to take exile. His intention was to uncover the psyche of especially the English people who were the colonizers of his region. In an "Introduction" to Fanon's *The Wretched of the Earth*, Jean Paul Sartre states that there is nothing more consistent than a racist humanism since the European has only been able to become a man through creating slaves and monsters. We find this phenomenon in Lamming's experience in exile. Before discussing Lamming's exploration for the Caribbean identity in Europe and America, I would like to trace that he travelled different African countries to identify the Caribbean's relationship with them, to dig the uprooted root of his ancestors. This chapter will concentrate on the political and cultural aspects of the Caribbean identities.

Racialized Identity at Home and Abroad:

In colonial context, body is a space through which a subject's essential identity is constructed. In "Introduction to 1984 edition", Lamming remarks that *The Pleasures of Exile* (1960) sought to reflect and interpret the anxieties and aspirations of a Caribbean sensibility at home and abroad. To start with the perspective of 'Racism', it is a form of identity politics with body colour. It is, at its heart, the belief that the human species is constituted by a number of separate and distinct biologically discrete sub-species: i.e., races. Lamming criticizes the fact that Europe argued and continues to argue that the Caribbean's black body is 'ugly, graceless and without history' (6). Again, Darwin in *The Origin of Species* claims that human being has evolved from 'ape' and it is often assumed that the first man of the world originated from Africa.

In his "Introduction", Lamming says, "this book is based upon facts of experience" (12). To apply the 'theory of evolution' in the context of the Caribbean, many of whom were originated from Africa, in "A Way of Seeing" Lamming narrates such a myth-based project of a fellow named Sam Selvon who had been asked to interview a poor Jamaican who was utterly disorganized in feeling by something happened to him in abroad, i.e., England:

> Sam related one incident that had to do with English factory girls creeping up behind the Jamaican, trying to lift his jacket in the hope of discovering his tail. The Jamaican peasant was deeply shaken by this reduction of his person to the status of an ape. They had colonized him by their particular kind of interest; and he was too scared to realize that those girls knew he had no tail. (78)

Racism works purely ideologically in this circumstance; and the English girls' gaze has undermined this black Caribbean's confidence and identity as a human being. In accordance with Althusser's view, he is interpellated as a subhuman subject, though he does not accept this degrading subjectivity. Again, racism seems to ascribe the English whites a sense of freedom to research on an immigrant black Caribbean anyway they like. Lamming states that actually "they were looking for something else [fantastic genital erection] which was there, which they had received from a traditional mythology, and which they felt was worth investigating" (78). From psychoanalytic view, it is a projection of the white girls' desire for a black phallus. Thus, the Caribbean man possesses a demanding identity for the *id* of the English girls. But their colonial *super ego* determines their *ego* over a colonized man. By commenting ironically on their curiosity as "a perfectly decent expression of desire between a woman and a man" (*78)*—Lamming has deconstructed the established Eurocentric binary-assumptions of the English versus the Caribbean, the white versus the black, and the colonizer versus the colonized, the superior versus the inferior; and in a way, has uplifted the Caribbean identity before the English female unconscious.

On the other hand, Lamming has related the Caribbean's racialized identity at home merely with poverty: "To be black, in the West Indies, is to be poor; whereas to be black (rich or poor) in an American context is to be a traditional target for specific punishments. Racism is not just an American problem. It is an element of American culture. No such thing is true of the British West Indies" (33). He adds: "In relation to the … American Negro and to Western culture he is, in a sense, a peripheral man". The most significant in his case is identity crisis: "The charge that he does not know who and what he is can be regarded as … a universal characteristic of his time" (34).

According to Michel Foucault's theory of 'gaze', our identity is constructed by how we are seen. At the very beginning of "A Way of Seeing", Lamming too has written—"I do believe that what a person thinks is very much determined by the way that person sees. This book is really no more than a report on one man's way of seeing, using certain facts of experience as evidence and guide … I am going to consider one or two things about colour as it affects black men living in a white society" (56); the way Fanon narrates in *Black Skin White Masks*. He goes on to review his sharing a flat with a black West Indian in Hampstead where both were expecting some important letters. But when they got letters addressed to someone named Singleton, they were convinced that their letters had been misdelivered to Singleton and went there to ask for those letters from an old white woman:

'So sorry,' the old woman said, 'I've looked at all the envelopes that came in for the last few days; and I didn't notice any BLACK stamps.'... She didn't simply mean Negro; she meant stamps marked Africa or India, China, or the West Indies. One kind, honest and courteous old woman had fixed almost two-thirds of the world's population with one word. (57)

To me, it also seems like Althusser's concept of 'interpellation', i.e., the calling into being of the subject by ideology. Here, she is subjectivising all the blacks of the world through the racist gaze.

Lamming discusses another subtle occurrence of racial discrimination, which the Caribbean would have been made aware of during the last few years of 1950s. For instance, when he is invited to America as a black writer, he is frequently reminded by an American lady about how he feels in America, like Fanon in France. In his words, "a man is always resident in the castle of his skin" (75). To Fanon, skin colour is an inseparable and inescapable entity for a race. However, Lamming proposes its logical solution to other black Caribbean, in his discussion about exile in England:

We must accept that racial antagonism in Great Britain is … an atmosphere and a background against which my life and yours are being lived. Our duty is to find ways of changing the root and perspectives of that background, of dismantling the accumulated myth, both cultural and political, which an inherited and uncritical way of seeing has now reinforced. And our biggest weapon, our greatest and safest chance lies in education: education among the young. (76)

Indeed, this manifests his quest for reconstructing the Caribbean racialized identity.

In *Black Skin White Masks,* Fanon says, "… the fact of the juxtaposition of the white and black races has created a massive psycho-existential complex" (12). Lamming's communication with a white Englishman during working in the B.B.C. is another evidence of racial degradation of the Caribbean in mid twentieth century world. Losing his way between Holborn and the Strand, Lamming approached some Englishmen for direction—

'Which way to the nearest Tube?' I asked.

'Keep straight ahead, sir,' one of them said.

Turn left! Keep straight ahead! These were contradictory guides … So I took the advice of the police …

'You thought I was lying,' he said.

'Not necessarily,' I said. '… I just wasn't sure.'

'I just want to tell you,' he said, 'that *I will never speak to a coloured man again.*' (90)

As Frantz Fanon says in his book *Black Skins White Masks*--'It is the racist who creates his inferior' (3). Here, the misunderstanding has injected a generalized racial prejudice and identity in the white psyche. And the victim reviews this attitude as nothing but the part of a privileged way of feeling in nearly every British people who treated blacks in general as 'others'. Even there is no wish for 'brothering the other' as Aphra Behn's *Oroonoko*. Additionally, disbelief is just putting one brick after another between the races and consequently the Western assumption of 'liberal humanism' is lost. Lamming does not want to allow the man's descendants to grow in such "a state of tragic and mindless illusion" (91). From existential philosophical perspective, he seems to hope that the Caribbean's essence of blackness should not precede their existence in the world. Furthermore, Lamming also explores new ways of changing the relationships between the colonizer and the colonized by creating new levels of understanding which will liberate them. This preoccupation is what I would call Lamming's 'way of seeing', his vision as delineated in his literary and creative explorations.

To Lamming, unlike the English, the Americans are very frank about the facts of racial judgments. Before analyzing it, I would like to focus on his conscious or unconscious tribute to America before glorification of self-identity as a recognized black Caribbean writer in "The African Presence": "It was white America who had invited me; it was white America who had received me. And it was white America who was going to support my stay" (190). Again, he expresses that if he had no Guggenheim Foundation support, he would not have been of any importance in the gaze of the elite American

Negroes. Indeed, this is a hegemonic ideology which the white world had won over the black Caribbean imagination. He thinks that as a black writer if he had gone to America from West Indies, instead of from England, he might not have been received so cordially. At this point, the Caribbean identity is contextual and subject to change.

Lamming then critically narrates his experience in that country which constructs his identity merely on the basis of his colour. He was received at airport in America with suspicion and interrogation. He includes, "… I had telephoned the evening I arrived [USA]; and I knew that between the interval of my telephoning my American publishers and my meeting with one of the editors, a list of hotels had already been drawn up, the most appropriate—noting my profession, my visiting status and my colour.…" (190)

Again, Lamming describes how a black Caribbean writer in America is always considered to be a poor other, although he might be "ambitious and bright" (196). He maintains that at the 27 Bar a white American started bullying him into talk about Lamming. That racist had an unerring instinct for spotting a non-American Negro and his feeling towards the American. We can trace the hegemony from his questions to Lamming:

'What do you write?'

'Books.'

'About what?'

'Us.' [As every writer should do to assert his national identity]

'In what style?' [As if the Caribbean has no style]

'Mine.'

'Have you had anything published?'

'Everything that is worth publishing.'

He paused; and fraternity certainly didn't reside in the irritated firmness of his jaw. (200)

That racist American refused to have even a drink with Lamming, a black Caribbean. Lamming ends this section with deconstruction of such a racialized Caribbean identity—"… Negro or not, my blood rebelled against the colossal myth which, in rewarding their ambitions, had fatally impoverished their spirit" (203). In fact, as a writer he has demolished the myth of the Caribbean inferiority by writing. His stance is that his nation has contributed much in the successful building of America, its culture and literature. Furthermore, in "Ishmael at Home", he tries to draw a similarity between the West Indies and America for some plurality in both. But the difference is that the Americans are united, while the Caribbean are disunited which is an obstacle to develop their identity.

Lamming goes on with the American's racial experimentation of him as a black Caribbean. In the same essay, he narrates his visit with an American family in Georgia. After his return to Manhattan, an American Negro asked him with an emphasis—"Where did you sleep?" When Lamming replied that he "was put in the room next to hers" (daughter of the family), the enquirer was "grateful for the clue to this mysterious invitation [of Lamming] to spend a week" there. "You know why he put the daughter next to you?"--he asked Lamming and answered himself--"You were put there to see whether the [white] daughter had a taste for niggers" (207). Here we have to keep in mind that 'nigger' is the slang word for a Negro/black. Lamming is "wondered" at the humiliating discovery of such a racialized identity of the Caribbean in America.

Implication of a binary opposition always operates as a mechanism behind the Caribbean's racialized identity. Lamming concludes this essay with his friend Blair's first tragic experience of the absolute barrier between white and black in the American South. Blair was a black and Piggy was a white who had known each other quite well at school; but it is a chameleon-like democracy which at once binds and separates these boys. Many years later, Blair saw piggy at the airport while both were going to America and greeted each other- "Forgetful of distance or time they had arranged their own entertainment with chess … for this flight had become a slow journey back to their original classroom" (209). However, when the plane landed at Miami in America,

They entered the restaurant, took a seat, and went on talking ... the waitress arrived ... 'You can't sit here,' the woman said ... both boys moved together in search of another table. Now she looked at Piggy and explained: 'You can stay, but your friend will have to go over there.' And she left them standing, silent and bewildered ... they had known colour prejudice, for the democracy of their school was never allowed to prolong itself into their social life; but they had never imagined this aspect of racism. They had never thought of colour as a kind of wall, a distance which could not be closed by individual choice in personal relationships ... Each would have liked to wish the other good luck; but they couldn't talk, speech had lost its power. Nothing could be said after that ominous noise: Good-bye. (209-210)

In 'Journey to an Expectation", Lamming has depicted the racial gaze on the Caribbean students in Oxford and Cambridge: "They notice a cold stare, an enigmatic sneer, the built-in compliment which is used to praise, and at the same time remind them who and what they are" (218). Towards the end, he says that a black man is colonized "by the agonizing assault of the other's eye whose meanings are based on a way of seeing he vainly tries to alter" (229). But in "The African Presence", he subverts the racial overgeneralization with an outstanding Caribbean figure Alex who works at University College, Ibadan in Oxford as a medical research Fellow: "Oxford helps, and he in turn helps Oxford ... science does not belong to Oxford any more than it belongs to Alex" (183). Thus Lamming sets a potential Caribbean idol before his subsequent generations to glorify the Caribbean identity.

Meanwhile, in "Caliban Orders History", Lamming revisits the colonial history and states that before decolonial movement even the Caribbean hybrid race or Mulattos, born of black mothers and hated by whites, "retained an attitude of superiority to the Blacks" (127). Then he indicates, with the reference to Toussaint's fruitless effort to harmonize the blacks and the mulattos by Dessalines, that such racial breach between them disempowered the Caribbean liberation movement. So he seems to encourage the racial harmony of his nation to assert a dignified Caribbean identity.

In fact, racism is pertinent to the rise of colonialism. The present day population of the Caribbean consists of a variety of racial groups all more or less in ancestral exile and all still subject to the hegemonic pressures of their former European owners and subsequently the American. That is to say, it is inextricable from the need of European colonialist and American neocolonialist powers to establish dominance over the Caribbean and justify it in the camouflage of 'civilization'. Since there is a legacy of racial myth behind all the above forms of the contemporary prejudices about the Caribbean in the world, Lamming tries to present his nation the reality about them and ideologically subvert the racial paradigms characteristic of the West.

Diasporic and Hybridized Caribbean Identity:

The huge diaspora and hybridity raise the obvious question of the Caribbean's national and political identity and vulnerability of exploitation. The process of colonization itself is a "radical diasporic movement" (Ashcroft: 2004). Now, to colonize a country involves leaving one's homeland, conquering another country, and imposing authority over it; thus colonization involves displacement and settlement of millions of people over the entire world along with the creation of new trans-cultural forms within the contact-zone. The colonizers' first weapon to destroy the Caribbean nationality and individuality was to create hybridity. As a result, the most significant feature of West Indian life and imagination since decolonization has been its sense of rootlessness; of neither belonging to the Caribbean landscape where they are, nor Africa or Asia where they originally came from. It creates their sense of identity crisis.

To identify the root of the rootlessness or dispossession of the Caribbean, Lamming has re-evaluates the diasporic evolution and contemporary devaluation of the Caribbean. The history of the Caribbean is dominated by the history of sugar, which is inseparable from the history of diasporic labour forces, especially from Africa, China, and India. Lamming states that "colonisation has one certain psychological result. The colonized is slowly and ultimately separated from the original ground where the colonizer found him ... it is precisely this awareness which undermines his confidence in what he really was and what he could really be" (157). In another instance he adds, "Nobody know where they sail from" (19). From this perspective, we can deduce that the Caribbean historical identity is not about root, but about route.

In "Ishmael at Home", Lamming rewrites and reminds his nation about their ancestors' who "traveled through the purgatory of the middle passage. However present the echoes of slavery, these West Indians [who returned the journey to West African landscape] have lost the chains which held their ancestors, ankle by ankle, mile after mile, through that night of exile, from the African coast to the Caribbean cradle" (155).

As a result of diaspora, a hybrid nation has been created here throughout five hundred years. Lamming says—"It is the brevity of the West Indian's history and the fragmentary nature of the different cultures which have fused to make something new" (35). His "In the Beginning" is a classic example of the Caribbean's diasporic and hybrid identity explicitly along with the disclosure of the colonizers' implicit identity at a glance:

> ... European descent, urged by adventure and greed ... [appeared] in this Caribbean Sea ... The indigenous Carib and Arawak Indians ... gradually disappear in a blind, wild forest of blood. That mischievous gift, the sugar cane, is introduced, and a fantastic human migration moves to the New world of the Caribbean; deported crooks and criminals, defeated soldiers and Royalist gentlemen fleeing from Europe, slaves from the West Coast of Africa, East Indians, Chinese, Corsicans and Portuguese. The list is always incomplete, but they ... meet on an unfamiliar soil, in a violent rhythm of race and religion. Today their descendants exist in an unpredictable and infinite range of custom and endeavour ... the most haphazard combinations, surrounded by memories of misery.... (17)

In repetition, an amalgamation of races leads to their sense of rootlessness and identity crisis. To locate from "Evidence and Example", we find some implicit trace of cultural hybridity, during the funeral of the dead George IV, in the behaviour of a West Indian who proves to have lost his self-esteem when he wears the regalia, here the sign of the colonizers.

In postcolonial theory, hybridity has become a touchstone for debates over colonial discourse and post-colonial identity. In the Caribbean context, it is inextricably related to racialized identity. In "Ishmael at Home", Lamming refers to the origin of his nation: "From the very beginning we were part of the island of China, and the island of Africa and the island of India ... we have not solved any racial questions; for prejudice is with us in one form or another; but we have been for a very long time a good example of the evolution of human relations in the future" (154). This view is apparent also in his review of the Caribbean history in "Caliban Orders History" where we come across the fact that the national heroic figure Toussaint's "troops were made up of Blacks, Mulattos, whites. They represented a possible future which san Domingo could be, united and without the inhibitions of race" (137). Ultimately "colour was losing its traditional learning of inferior and debased; for the ex-slaves had gained a new confidence" (145), he comments. The implication is that, though the Caribbean races are hybridized, they have to learn from history that racial unity is most significant for the destiny of their nation.

As "In the Beginning" portrays, the association of Bob, Singh and Lee is a metonymy of the Caribbean hybrid identity, standing for three major national groups, Afro-Caribbean, Indian and Chinese, who struggle to maintain their close friendship and plan an agenda for the future. In spite of their having diversity of complexion and coming from three different parts of the world, "they speak the same idiom, live the same history" (18). And the Creole-English form used in these West Indians' conversation is an abrogation of Standard English and thereby a perfect manifestation of the Caribbean hybrid identity through language. Significantly enough, it is to the younger generation that Lamming delivers the task of a different kind of education from the colonial one. Here an imaginary English Lady is shown as being educated by the story of these Tribe Boys, disseminated by the children. It is a remarkable counter-discursive stance of Lamming in the sense that the descendants of slaves are now teaching a descendant of colonial masters their dialectical history from the Caribbean perspective. Lamming notes their conversation as:

'Who are these Tribe Boys,' the Lady asks.

'Tis some history 'bout San Cristobal,' says Bob. 'We learn it from early.'

'An' if any strangers around,' said Singh, 'sometimes we tell it as a work. 'Cause not everybody know how to tell it.' (18)

Thus, Lamming situates his own tale, like that of the boys, as a 'work' of labour offered to those who do not yet know of an almost extinct civilization, the vestiges of which remain in the legends and lore of the later survivors. He considers the legends and fables to be the work of the imagination and he offers them as a creative alternative to the distorted history of the Caribbean.

Lamming comments on a relevant issue in "The Occasion for Speaking":

> The West Indian student ... should not be sent to England ... because the student's whole development as a person is thwarted by the memory ... which has been maintained and fertilized by the England's historic ties with the West Indies ... In England ... all relationships begin with an assumption of previous knowledge, a knowledge acquired in the absence of the people known. (25)

I have found it useful here to include that Lamming bears a resemblance to Michel Foucault's notion of Eurocentric discourse, as described by him in *The Archaeology of Knowledge,* in dismantling the colonizers' politics to identify the colonized Caribbean. Again, Lamming has deconstructed such prejudice about the Caribbean identity in his counter-discursive assertion:

> Colonialism is the very 'base and superstructure' [as Marxism] of the West Indian's cultural awareness ... What the West Indian has to do if he is going to be released from this prison of colonialism ... is precisely what the whole world is now called upon to do ... For the West Indies—African, Chinese and Indian by mixture—by the boys Singh, Lee and Bob—belong to that massive peasant majority whose leap in the twentieth century has shattered all the traditional calculations of the West, of European civilization. (36)

Edward Said in *Culture and Imperialism* also situates Lamming as one of the key figures in the transition from colonization to decolonization. To Said, his works belong to an important body of 'resistance culture'. Said further claims that the voices of such writers are not only integral part of political movement, but in many ways the movement's '*successfully*' guiding imagination, intellectual and figurative energy reseeing and rethinking the terrain common to whites and non-whites.

The West Indian cricket team of 1950 at Lords in England is used as a metaphor of the Caribbean hybrid identity. In Lamming's words—"Indian, Negro, Chinese, White, Portuguese mixed with Syrian ... the mixtures are as weird and promising as the rainbow. And the combination of that team is not a political gimmick. That is the West Indian team; for it is, in fact, the West Indian situation"

(37). By celebrating the victory of the West Indian cricket team against a mother country, Lamming glorifies the Caribbean identity.

Exile as a Quest for the Caribbean (Literary) Identity:

Literature is a powerful medium of establishing one's identity. In his long and detailed editorial "Introduction" to *The Islands In Between,* Louise James comments about the exile of the West Indian writers and critics during 1950s and 1960s—"Seen against the various tensions of the area, it is not surprising that many creative Caribbean writers moved away from the West Indies to see their predicament in perspective". From Lamming's argument, we can say that it was due to their "hunger for recognition" of being a writer from a neglected area, hunger for asserting a distinguished Caribbean literary identity before the world. According to *Encyclopedia of post-colonial Literatures in English,* the perspective provided by distance prompts these expatriate writers to define their racial, cultural and national identity through opposition to white society and its value system. This chapter will concentrate on the experience of Lamming and some Caribbean writers like Mais, Hoszer, Selvon etc. who chose deliberate exile in England and America during 1950s as their search for the Caribbean identity as well as the assertion of themselves as the Caribbean literary genius. I would scrutinize their experiences.

By confronting and in some cases challenging the Eurocentric prejudices about themselves, these expatriate writers attempted to promote the Caribbean identity beyond its degrading attributes imposed by the Western discourse and hegemony. By the way, almost every one of them makes his allegorical voyages into the hinterland of the self for fulfillment. Lamming identifies all of them with a historically aware resistant community of creative writers, scholars and activists from the Caribbean—"that started as an alternative to the old and privileged Prospero, too old and too privileged to pay attention to the needs of his own native Calibans" (152).

Again, the experience of exile in England, though it disillusioned and crushed these immigrants, gave them a new insight, a new appreciation and identity with their island. It seems that for Lamming, emigration is on one level a form of self-exploration, a process of re-assessing and evaluating one's identity, as well as a process of self-knowledge which the emigrants must acquire in order to overcome the colonial syndrome that makes them hanker after other landscapes. The detachment and self-searching afforded by emigration enable them to have a better perception of themselves as well as their landscapes, and as an experience, it provides them with a certain impetus and drive for political (re)action.

In Lamming's view, the Caribbean artists are compelled to move beyond the confines of history and experience, to explore new alternatives and possible meanings even in a history of displacement, slavery, and subjugation. In a sardonic passage of his seminal analysis of the writer-in-exile, he justifiably asserts: "The [names of the] West Indian novelists living in a state of chosen exile … make temporary noise in the right West Indian circles. Their books have become handy broomsticks which the new nationalist will wave at a foreigner who asks the rude question: 'What can your people do except doze?'" (46).

Lamming claims: "the discovery of the novel by West Indians as a way of investigating and projecting the inner experiences of the West Indian community [is an] important event in our history" (41). Particularly, he proves himself as a part of the Caribbean literary identity when an American publisher buys his *In the Castle of My Skin*. He also refers to a West Indian named Alexander Hamilton, the federal guy, who "contributed so richly to their [American] constitutional literature … C. L. R. James lectured in the universities of America, both north and south … Eric Williams … as a professor of Howard University" (154). Thus, he wants to indicate that a Caribbean literature is emerging with its own voice, confident enough to make use of writing to articulate a distinctly Caribbean vision.

Again, Lamming outlines not only what the West Indian writers have gained from the English, but also the contribution made by the West Indian writers to English fiction. Adjunct to that is his famous statement--"English is a West Indian language". In reality, the location of so many Caribbean writers in London at that time ultimately enabled them a clearer sense of a developing Caribbean literature along with a national consciousness--which are significant aspects of their glorification of the Caribbean identity: "No Barbadian, no Trinidadian, no St Lucian, no islander from the West Indies

69

sees himself as a West Indian until he encounters another islander in a foreign country … In this sense most West Indians of my generation were born in England" (214).

In "A Way of Seeing", Lamming reasserts the Caribbean identity through artistic creativity. As a poet he was invited to the Institute of Contemporary Arts in England in 1950: "I was simply an anonymous West Indian emigrant who could read and who, mysterious as it might seem [to the English gaze], had even trespassed on the territory of the literate who made fame by writing" (60). The prejudiced English outlook considers it as a "black courage". But Lamming indicates that black courage in the face of language was pure black magic; and magic, black or white, is not easy to accept.

As the title signifies, the discursive spaces of *The Pleasures of Exile* shift continually from multiple sites of marginality—London, North America, Africa and the Caribbean—contesting old notions of self-identity and destabilizing generic margins. In West Africa and in the United States, the authorial persona is the travelling colonial who measures, for example, the cultural meaning and political implication of his covering the funeral of King George VI for the BBC Caribbean programme. Driving also from Kumasi to Zaria, or exploring Harlem, there is a pronounced sense of his contributing to a Caribbean destiny.

In fact, exile of the Caribbean writers is a journey with an expectation for deconstructing, reconstructing and popularizing their literary identity. Out of this conviction and commitment, Lamming regards the West Indian writer's books as "his country's cultural exports to the world beyond the West Indies. That is how Europe and America … China and India would know them. They would be seen as the creative products of a particular community at a particular time" (42). It is vivid here that "a particular community at a particular time" implies the colonized Caribbean nation which no more needs to learn 'civility' from the Western enlightening nations. To uphold his assertion, he himself exemplifies—"after re-reading this history [*Black Jacobins*] of the Haitian Revolt it is clear to me that, level for level, generation for generation, there was no British intellectual of the thirties who had a finer mind than James" (47).

Again, Lamming glorifies the West Indian artistic ingenuity through an account of his visit as a guest to America, Harlem. There in a speech, the Master of the ceremony to a Bar's opening announced repeatedly, to Lamming's astonishment—"we were honoured to have here ... the world's greatest living author [Lamming] ... I got up and briefly raised my right arm in a natural show of a victory, our victory" (197). To have made this recognition in a region where doing something praiseworthy by a black had always been regarded as impossibility, is a significant achievement by Lamming on behalf of the Caribbean literary identity.

In brief, each of the exiled writers has posed new and complex challenges in *The Pleasures of Exile* to approach the Caribbean identities and origins, to express one's self creatively before the world readers and thus contribute to the national reconstruction.

Conclusion:

Lamming concludes his "Introduction" with—"this book is a report on one man's way of seeing" (13). From Foucault's idea of 'gaze', we can deduce that *The Pleasures of Exile* is about Lamming's way of perceiving the Caribbean identities—how the world sees them and they see or should see themselves, how their identity is constructed by canonical discourses and how they are affected by that in the world, how far they conform to and confronts with that stereotype etc. But since his report is based on a single vision or perspective, his innovation of the Caribbean identity is subjective and relative to particular times and spaces. So he cannot demand absolute authenticity or universality. Yet he deserves authority to assert it for being a Caribbean eyewitness.

Again, to define 'the Caribbean' is--to characterize, to describe the nature and stature of the nation, making it clear, stating precisely its meaning, making it become more vivid. But defining the Caribbean in such terms has been particularly problematic for the Caribbean writers. This is because the problems of definition have to do with the problems of a broken history and a discontinuity in culture. And the history of the Caribbean has been perpetually marked by the annihilation of natives, diaspora, after-effects of conquest, slavery, repression, colonialism and resistance; thus hindering their historical and cultural continuity. The uprooting of the natives and importation of African slaves to toil in sugar plantations, the introduction of Indian indentured laborers to replace African slaves after the abolition of slavery, as well as the presence of European colonizers led to the creation of hybrid communities of immigrants or exiled, all with broken cultures and history. Subsequently it resulted in what is commonly referred to as the 'melting pot' situation that brought people of myriad cultural and linguistic backgrounds together without the real cohesion what could unify them. Therefore, they suffer from identity crisis. Still, the memory of alienation, dislocation, indignity, loss and dispossession of cultural base create a kind of self-awareness—which might have inspired Lamming to exile for re(dis)covering the Caribbean identity, for "learning to be a [dignified] Caribbean person" (*Personal Interview*).

Meanwhile, the Caribbean identity is sometimes problematic for its hybrid or hyphenated identities. For instance, the Afro-Caribbean implies a subject's dual heredity; i.e., African past and Caribbean present. In other words, their belonging to a no-man's-land leads to their sense of rootlessness and identity crisis. They belong to various cultures syncretically, but uniquely to none and accepted by none. So, the region seems to be a contact zone where people lacked a homogenous entity. Yet, in *The Pleasures of Exile*, Lamming explores new visions and meanings of the Caribbean experiences, and attempts his historical sketch of the nation's identity. He writes from a point of view inside a historical process, and awareness is all. He also dismantles the facts of--how people born in this Third World are frequently victimized as the descendants of sub-human species by the First world ideology, discourses, media, and the politics of racial myths; being filled with a sense of fear, insecurity, inferiority and so on—leading to identity crisis. His stance is that—by relooking, upholding and celebrating the Caribbean history and by counter-discursive writings against canonical discourses, they can fight back the alienation and racial antagonism, and reconstruct the sense of their nationalistic identity. For Lamming, nationalism appears to be a prerequisite to political freedom because it nourishes the Caribbean identity with glory and pride that enable him to reconstruct his nation.

In my research, I have tried to prove that the colonial discourses have constructed the Caribbean identity with lots of negative myths throughout centuries to sustain their colonial 'civilizing mission'. So Lamming's ever creative instinct drives him to "choose a way to change the meaning and perspective of this ancient tyranny" (229). Thus, *The Pleasures of Exile* has fulfilled the criteria for a 'counter-discourse' indicated in my title—in that, it seeks to deconstruct significations of authority and power exercised in, e.g., a canonical text *The Tempest*, to release its stranglehold on allegorical representation of the Caribbean and, by implication, to intervene in hegemonic conditioning of their identity. His message is for those Caribbean who suffer from identity crises in different contexts. His quest is to stimulate the Caribbean consciousness to assess their history, culture and identity not through the gaze of others, as W.E.B.Du Boise's "Double-Consciousness" alerts, but to justify from the Caribbean perspectives. He emphasizes counter-discourse's potential to define national culture, and the need for a distinguished Caribbean literature against canonical discourse. Furthermore, in order to create nationalism among the Caribbean, he enables the Caribbean to transcend their history of humiliation, and recreates the Caribbean history of resistance by revisioning it from pre-colonial state to the emergence of decolonization in 1960s.

It is remarkable that on the way to discover the identity of the black Caribbean, he has uncovered the camouflaged identity of the white Europeans and Americans. To improve the Caribbean's cultural designation and self-determination, Lamming lays bare the political, cultural and psychological damages; while also exploring new ways of overcoming these barriers to assert a dignified national identity: "In the Caribbean we have a glorious opportunity of making some valid and permanent contribution to man's life in this century" (50). Finally he clarifies his objective that "this book … is directed to my generation throughout the Caribbean, irrespective of language, race or political status" (225). Since he has assessed the Caribbean from both inside and outside the region, born in West Indies and exiled in London, like Rushdie's "Imaginary Homelands", he is privileged to represent the Caribbean identity. Finally, I would like to put forward that—by dismantling the textual unconscious of *The Tempest* as a poststructuralist critic and rejecting the stereotype identities created by other legitimizing imperial discourses, *The Pleasures of Exile* functions as a counter-discursive signifier of the post-colonial Caribbean's metamorphosis into some cross-cultural identities, identities that are experienced between the Caribbean and the West.

Notes

[1] See, for example, Mead and Campbell. Eds, *Shakespeare's Books: Contemporary Cultural Politics and the Persistence of Empire* (1993).

[2] For a persuasive account of how the study of English Literature contributed to the socio-political consolidation of the British Empire, see, for example, Viswanathan's *Masks of Conquest: Literary Study and British rule in India* (1989).

[3] See, for further information, Bill Ashcroft's *Post-colonial Transformation: Interpolation.*

Works Cited

Anderson, Benedict. <u>Imagined Communities: Reflections on the origin and rise of</u>

    <u>nationalism</u>. London: n.p., 1982. Print.

Ashcroft, Bill, Gareth Griffiths, and Helen Tiffin. Eds. <u>The Empire Writes Back:</u>

    <u>Theory and Practice in Post-colonial Literatures</u>. London: Routledge, 1989. Print.

----------. <u>Key Concepts in Post-Colonial Studies</u>. London and New York: Routledge, 2004.

    Print.

----------. <u>The Post- colonial Studies Reader</u>. London: Routledge, 1995. Print.

Azim, Firdous. "Whose English Is It Anyway? Problems of Identity and National

    Language". Zaman, Niaz. Ed. <u>Essays on Commonwealth Writing</u>. Dhaka: The University

    Press, 1991. Print.

Balderston, Daniel, and Mike Gonzalez. Ed. <u>Encyclopedia of Latin American And</u>

    <u>Caribbean Literature 1900-2003</u>. London: Routledge, 2004. Print.

Benson, Eugene, and L.W.Conolly. Ed. <u>Encyclopedia of Post-colonial Literatures in</u>

    <u>English</u>. Vol.1. Print.

Boehmer, Elleke. <u>Colonial & Postcolonial Literature</u>. Oxford and New York: Oxford

    University Press, 1995. Print.

Brooker, Peter. <u>A Glossary of Cultural Theory</u>. London: Arnold, 2003. Print.

Burnett, Paula. Ed. <u>The Penguin Book of Caribbean Verse</u>. Middlesex: Penguin, 1986. Print.

Childs, Peter, and R.J.Patrick Williams. <u>An Introduction to Post-Colonial Theory</u>. England:

    Pearson Education Limited, 1997. Print.

Clawson, David L. <u>Latin America and the Caribbean: Lands and Peoples</u>. New York:

McGraw-Hill, 2004. Print.

Cudjoe, Selwyn R. "Identity and Caribbean Literature." Japan: Nara, June 24, 2001. Web.

accessed on May 08, 2008 < http:// Trinicenter.com>.

Donnell, Alison, and Sarah Lawson Welsh. Eds. The Routledge Reader in Caribbean

Literature. London and New York: Routledge, 1996. Print.

Fanon, Frantz. Black Skin White Masks. 1952. Markmann, Charles Lam. Trans. London:

MacGibbon and Kee, 1968. Print.

----------. The Wretched of the Earth: On National Culture. London: Penguin, 1963. Print.

Gandhi, Leela. Postcolonial Theory. New Delhi: Oxford University Press, 1998. Print.

Gilbert, Helen, and Joanne Tompkins. Post-colonial Drama: Theory, practice, politics.

London and New York: Routledge, 1996. Print.

Howarth, David. Discourse. New Delhi: Viva Books Private Limited, 2005. Print.

Lamming, George. The Pleasures of Exile. London: Allison & Busby, 1984. Print.

Lazarus, Neil. Ed. The Cambridge Companion to Postcolonial Literary Studies.

Cambridge: Cambridge University Press, 2004. Print.

Marshall, P.J. Ed. The Cambridge Illustrated History of the British Empire.

Cambridge: Cambridge University Press, 1999. Print.

Microsoft ® Encarta ® 2006. © 1993-2006 Microsoft Corporation.

Nair, Supriya M. Caliban's Curse: George Lamming and the Revisioning of History.

Ann Arbor: University of Michigan Press. <http:// www.books.google.com/>

Web. accessed on May 08, 2008.

Narasimhaiah, C D. Ed. "The West Indies". An Anthology of Commonwealth Poetry.

India: MacMillan, 2004. Print.

O'Reilly, Christopher. Post-Colonial Literature. Cambridge: Cambridge University Press,

2001. Print.

Randall, Stephen J., and Graeme S. Mount. The Caribbean Basin. London: Routledge, 1998.

Print.

Said, Edward W. Orientalism. New Delhi: Penguin, 2001. Print.

Sheller, Mimi. Consuming the Caribbean: From Arwaks to Zombies, 2003. Print.

Smith, Philip. Cultural Theory: An Introduction. Massachusetts and Oxford: Blackwell, 2001.

Print.

Walder, Dennis. Post-colonial Literatures in English: History Language Theory. Oxford:

Blackwell, 1998. Print.

Webster, Merriam. Encyclopedia of Literature. Massachusetts: Incorporated, 1995. Print.

Williams, Patrick, and Laura Chrisman. Eds. Colonial Discourse And Post-Colonial Theory.

England: Pearson Education Limited, 1994. Print.

Made in the USA
Coppell, TX
04 October 2021